'A Sooner Born'

I'm a Sooner born,
I'm a Sooner bred,
And when I die
I'll be a Sooner dead!

This is a compilation of the letters that my mother wrote to her parents during the Second World War, and the articles that she wrote about her life in Oklahoma (the Sooner State).

Sue Newton

Sue Newton

The portrait on the front cover is of my Mother and was painted by Robert Lyon who became Principal of the Edinburgh Royal College of Art from 1942-1960. He taught art to the Ashington group of miners and is portrayed in the play 'The Pitmen Painters'. He asked my Mother to sit for him in 1940 for this portrait as he wanted to practise painting the pose.

Copyright © Sue Newton

This book is published 2018 by Sue Newton Publishing.
The Court House, 24 South Road, Grassendale Park, Liverpool, L19 0LT.

Printed by Rayross Print Factory Limited.

S Newton has asserted her moral right to be identified as the author of this work in accordance with the Copyright, Design and Patents Act 1988.

ISBN 978-0-9544819-2-6

Book design: Izabella Newton
Photographic Editor: Chris Newton

This book is dedicated to the memory of my Mother.

Betty Bradbury née Elisabeth Galt

Contents

Prologue 7.

Participants 8.

Chapter 1.	A Sooner Born 1	11.
	A Bit Personal (Daily Ardmoreite)	22.
Chapter 2.	Anglicized at Last	25.
Chapter 3.	The Letters 1-34 to America 1939-45	35.
Chapter 4.	Post War Articles (No Time for Tears)	141.
Chapter 5.	'So you're an American!'	147.
Chapter 6.	A Sooner Born 2	155.

Epilogue 161.

Prologue

This book is about my Mother, it tells of her upbringing in mid-West America, in the state of Oklahoma, her student days at university, her marriage to my Father and her life with her husband and two small children during the 2nd World War years in the United Kingdom, all in her own words. She writes extremely well, giving an incredible insight into life in both America and the United Kingdom. She wrote articles about the history of Oklahoma and her own upbringing in pioneering America. The book starts with these; they show the pioneering spirit of America, her pioneering spirit in furthering her education at University, meeting and marrying an Englishman going to live in England and bringing up 2 small children.

She wrote regularly to her parents during World War Two, when Britain was fighting the Germans and it is these letters which are printed in Chapter 4. I am grateful to my American Grandmother for keeping her letters she received during the war and giving them to me. Their tone was always up beat, telling the domestic stories of bringing up her family and coping with the limitations of living in a war zone, but never complaining about her situation. Always reassuring her family back home in America that she is coping with whatever life throws at her. A few years after the war the Bradbury family went to live in Liverpool where my father was City Architect. My Mother gave many talks about life in England, and these are in chapter 6 along with details of her later life. This book is my tribute to her indomitable spirit.

Sue Newton, née Susan Bradbury.

Participants featured in the Letters

Elisabeth- Galt, born 1909 married Ronald Bradbury 12th May 1933 - Writer of the letters.

Mama – Rowena (Roie) Armstrong born in Georgia, was the 3rd wife of Lee Galt and mother of Elisabeth and Monroe.

Papa - Lee L Galt born in Georgia in 1852.
Father of Elisabeth

Mary Machen - step sister to Elisabeth.

Marie - step sister.

Monroe Galt – brother.

Ethelyn – wife of Monroe.

Ronald Bradbury - born 1910 married Betty (Elisabeth) 12th May 1933.

George Bradbury – father of Ronald, born 1873, died 1953.

Eva Bradbury (nee Symmons) – mother of Ronald, born 1869, died 1953.

Lee Bradbury- son of Ronald and Elisabeth born 2nd April 1935, died February 2018.

Susan Bradbury- daughter of Ronald and Elisabeth born 8th Dec 1938

Beattie (Surtees)- maid to the Bradbury family 1937- 1944, died Dec 2015.

The American Galt Family

Father of Papa; Edward Ballenger Machen GALT

Mother of Papa; Elizabeth Lowry McGHEE

Papa;
Leland Lewis 'Lee' Galt
B: 11 Oct 1858 Whitfield, Georgia
D: 1948 Carter, Oklahoma

Marriage 1882; Johanna CARNEY
Children;
Machen
Mary
John
Lena

Marriage 1897; Margaret Ellen CARNEY
Children;
Mildred

Marriage 1905; Rowena Elizabeth HAMTRON - FRANKLIN née ARMSTRONG (married Samuel B FRANKLIN, 1895)
Children;
Rowena & Samuel had;
Leonard
Rowena & Leland had;
Monroe Sanford
Elisabeth Rowena

Chapter One
A Sooner Born 1

Papa was an old man when I was born. I was the last child of his third marriage, which sounds rather indulgent on his part, but in fact was the natural sequence of the logical events in his life. His marriage to Mama was the culmination of his desire to replace his second Georgia peach by another Georgia peach.

It's a long story, so I had better start at the beginning, Papa was a young man among many brothers on a plantation in Georgia. The plantation was extensive and could have eventually given a livelihood to all of the brothers and their respective wives, but the Civil War intervened and when Sherman marched to the Sea his route was over their plantation: the houses were raised to the ground, the fields and trees burned, nothing was left but desolation and there was no future life for the young men of the family – without homes, labour or prospect.

The cry of "Go West Young Man" was the cry of the day and Papa went with two of his older brothers a long way West into what was known as Indian Territory. This was the land that the government had given to the Five Civilised Tribes of Indians (the Chickasaw, Chocktow, Cherokee, Creek and Seminoles), promising them that it was theirs to make up for the land that had been taken away from them in the East.

Here they could supposedly live according to their customs and not be crowded out by the White Men any more. The long trek for some of them through the lengthy journey from the East, meeting conflict practically all the way has been described by one of their artists in a heart-rending picture entitled "The Trail of Tears". Perhaps they could have been left alone if migrants from the devastation of Georgia and other states – like Papa and his friends - had not wanted a new life. Soon these migrants were infiltrating to such an extent that with their civilised ways they were over-riding the Indians in the development and peopling of Indian Territory.

Little towns which had begun as mere wide places in the roads became small towns with growing community life; the land was developing, and the Indians were being moved further and further into the corners of the Territory. My father and his brothers were the engineers of this new country. They built the roads, bridges, dams, buildings, schools and railways. The history of the state of Oklahoma is the history of their lives.

With so many white settlers in, they felt that they had to have official recognition for their entrance, but it wasn't until Harrison became president that the White population asked him to let the Indian Territory become the forty-sixth state of the Union. This request went before Congress and was granted, and Indian Territory became the forty-second state of the Union. The story goes that an imaginary line was drawn down the Eastern side of the Territory. All the would-be settlers lined up on the Eastern side and, at daybreak on the eventful day, a pistol was fired and the settlers raced to mark their claim, being able to own the land that they had so marked. Human nature being what it is, some were smarter than others and slipped through in the darkness of the previous night and laid better claims. In other words, they got there sooner than the others; hence Oklahoma has always been known as the 'Sooner State'. Its actual name is the Choctaw word for home of the red man.

Into this wild country Papa and his brother came, each with a young bride. Uncle John was the lawyer business man who became a Mayor at a later date. Papa was the self-taught civil engineer, who built the homes, the schools and the roads. With them was a Dr. Hardy who finally decided to settle in this new little town. Itinerant wagon-shops of cloth, haberdashery - and anything the pioneer women might need – were set up as little stores. Main Street was indeed a wide street, flanked by mostly single storey buildings, although the one hotel was two storeys high with a double porch running around the front. Here the men came in the evenings, or during work of the day, to meet friends or do business; sitting in the rocking chairs that lined the porch. There were scores of booted feet perched on the porch railing.

Cutting at right angles into this Main Street was a street called Cadda, named after a creek that ran outside town. This was the domain of the Indians who came to town each Saturday. As an Indian, whose land was lost in the Territory becoming a state, if his name was on the Indian Role, the Federal Government gave him regular money, which usually burnt his pocket or his hand to such an extent that he always spent it as soon as he got it. Caddo was full of all things that would appeal to Indians and was their gathering place in town.

Not only were there the Indians and the Whites, but also the Negroes who, after the deserved freedom granted them after the Civil War, were in a precarious state. After freedom, they were their own responsibility, especially in a newly admitted state where things had moved too quickly for there to be established law and order that could control so many human factors. Before the plantation masters (not all as bad as some literature would have us believe) saw to their housing, their little churches and schools for their offspring, now the towns had to do this and it took time to get organised.

Our town was divided into four wards, each with its own primary school – one ward being given over to the negroes with their own schools and teachers. The Junior High School and Senior High were in the centre of the town and all pupils of that age and standard from the three white wards came to these schools. Again, the Negroes had their own junior and senior high. Their parents crossed over into the white part of town, mainly to work either in the stores or the homes of white people. I had always been conscious of negroes as part of the background of my youth. Presumably the Civil War had cut off the negroes from the white families and made them independent - but for many generations to come, they still found their life and interests among the life and interests of the white people. My Mother and Father were good to the negroes who worked for them and helped them in more ways than one. The negroes relied upon them for the stability of their lives as my parents relied upon them for the embellishments of their daily tasks.

I think that one of the greatest enrichments of my life as a child was the number of coloured people who worked for us. For years there was Bertha the cook, much of my present philosophy of life I base upon that of Ole Bertha, who was massive in size of body and heart. If there was anything the matter with me, she would say, "Lawdsy, child - there ain't nothing worth frettin' over. Don't you fret." She didn't, and she always got there smiling. I can close my eyes even now and see Bertha making cream gravy to go with the fried chicken and, as she stirred the creamy sauce in her skillet, her shapely hips rotated to the rhythm of her spoon. Once I asked her, "Bertha, why do you have to waggle your hips as you stir the cream?" With a broad smile that broke all records she replied, "Away child, you can't make good, proper gravy unless you puts your hips into it."

After Bertha, who left to get married and later moved to California, our chief help for many years was Pet – short for Petunia, who was cook and her beautiful daughter Hallifay, a mulatto, who acted as maid. Pet too was beautiful, but the morals of her behaviour did not match the beauty of her body -her moral code did not meet her emotions and she was always in a domestic tangle. Officially she had been married to her first husband, but when she grew tired of him he departed from her little wooden house in negro town and his place was taken by another. When she worked for us she was 'on' her third common law husband. She was such a good worker and provider that the respective husbands did not feel the necessity for work. Eventually, Pet would kick them out. One day she asked Mama if she could put up a cot in the back hall and spend a few nights there. Mama asked "Why, Pet? Is there something the matter at home?" "Yes Mam," she replied. "I just kicked my last husband out and he said if I so much as looked at another man, he would fill my back full of lead." Mother gave her permission and for almost a week Pet did not stir from our house, until my Mother suggested that she go home to see how things were and to put her own house in order. "Yes'm" she said, "I'll 'phone my cousin who has an old jalopy to come fetch me." Soon there drove up to the door an old, open tourer without a top, with the door tied on with string. Pet climbed over and away she and her cousin went, both laughing heartily. They made a handsome couple. Some half an hour later, there was a call from the nearby White hospital. Were we the folks that employed Pet? If so, would we please come and make arrangements for her to be transported to the nearest Negro hospital. It seems that, when Pet and her cousin drew up in front of her house in Negro town, her latest husband was hiding behind a shrub in the front yard and, as Pet climbed over the side of the old car, the thwarted man fired a sawn-off shotgun, filling her back full of lead. He had kept his word, and beautiful Pet died on the way to hospital.

After Pet died, her equally beautiful daughter Hallifay took over her role. She was an ardent member of the local Coloured Baptist Church, singing in the choir. At this time, I was home from New York with my English fiancé. It was a Sunday night when Hallifay said, "Miz Galt, "could I go early tonight so I can be in good time for our church service? We hasn't paid our organist and she's going back to college this fall, and tonight's plate (collection) goes to her."

Mother answered, "Of course, Hallifay, you go now and put this in the plate for me" and handed her a dollar bill.

"Hallifay," Ronald asked "do they allow White people into your church? Could we come to hear you?"

"Why, yessir" she said, "Everybody's welcome."

Ronald and I got another couple and we got into the car and went across the railroad tracks into Negro town. We didn't know exactly where the church was, but you could hear the singing Blacks. It was a small one-roomed, wooden church with a little steeple. We mounted the three-plank steps and went into the church. It was a large bare room with a raised platform at one end. On the wooden benches sat the full congregation. They were swaying, murmuring their Hallelujahs as the Minister spoke. He was quite an old man, full of the wisdom of years and the beauty and belief of his soul. "De Lord am so big, I can't go round him." With arms stretched high, "De Lord am so tall I can't go over him." Then the arms pointed and hung down to the floor, "De Lord am so deep I can't go under Him. I just got to go through Him" and one very definite finger pointed a straight line in front of him." The amens were a wall of praise for his words.

But I have jumped the years. Let's go back to the pioneer days. I left Papa with his first bride.

It was a hard struggle those early days in Indian Territory and childbirth took its toll of many a young mother. Puerperal fever often followed a birth as night follows day. Papa's first wife bore him four children, but she died giving birth to the last. His second wife was again from Georgia, and she died giving birth to Papa's fifth child. He needed a wife for love, companionship and to make the house a home for his five children. He was determined that she, too, should come from Georgia. He wrote to his sister Meg in Georgia and asked if she would come look after the five while he made his way back to Georgia to look over the 'Crop of Belles'. Aunt Meg was only too pleased, as she was a widow by this time, and it would be a new life for her to soften her grief. She came, and Papa went to find another Georgia peach.

His journey East was not a success, for he found no one whom he wished to ask to be his third wife. He would turn to the Territory and let Meg, deputise as housekeeper. It was a long train journey from Georgia to Dallas. The only means of eating for the five days and nights was to disembark at each stop of the train. The stops were scheduled for breakfast, dinner and supper at little towns along the route where a certain foresighted Mr. Harvey had opened up eating houses: rough but ready. These Harvey Houses offered solace and comforts to the weary travellers. At Chattanooga, Tennessee, Papa was walking along the depot platform when he saw an old friend from Georgia. "Why, Armstrong, what are you doing here?" he asked.

"I might well ask you the same thing, Lee Galt." Beside him was a lovely full-blown young lady with a small two year old boy by her side.

"This is my daughter Roie" Mr. Armstrong said. "She's just lost her husband in a diphtheria epidemic in Alabama and I am putting her on the train for Dallas, where she is going to start a new life. Where are you going? Wouldn't be Dallas?"

Papa answered, "It is, and I would be mighty proud to keep my eye on her and see she doesn't get up to any mischief." I don't need to tell you the sequel to this conversation. Papa kept his eye glued to her. Her youth (she was twenty years younger than he), her beauty, her motherhood, her being from Georgia originally and the daughter of his old friend - these made her the ideal candidate for 'third wife'. When he asked her on the last day before they got to Dallas, she wisely said that she would like a testing time. "Mr. Galt," she said "You go on back to Indian Territory and I'll stay in Dallas and open my little millinery shop. Give me six months, and then you'll know my answer."

The answer, at last, was "Yes". Papa brought five children to the marriage and Mama brought one. I often wondered if she knew exactly what she was taking on, but she turned out to be a very unusual and helpful stepmother. Her oldest stepdaughter was only a few months younger than she was. She was liked and accepted by them all –

except Aunt Meg. It was only natural that Aunt Meg would feel that Papa no longer needed her and her role was obsolete. By the time my whole brother and I were born Aunt Meg had taken up her home with Aunt Bess who, by this time, had come with her family into Indian Territory. There was only one drawback. Meg wouldn't acknowledge my mother, maintaining that she would never speak to her, or to the two children of the marriage. This meant that, although Aunt Bess' home where Aunt Meg lived, was only across the street to us, she would never speak to us, although my mother had taught us always to greet her. When there was a family collection to buy Aunt Meg a birthday present, we always contributed our share, but there was never any acknowledgement of the fact.

She was a most interesting character, Aunt Meg. She had sixty snow white curls, cascading onto her shoulders. The story was told, that only once in her life had she had the heavy curls put up, and that was on her wedding day. The weight of them on her head gave her such a headache that she promised her husband she would never attempt to pile them up again. In their married life in Georgia in the Civil War, she played an important role in an act of bravery when she saved their little town. This role entitled her to be a resident in the Confederate Home years later in our Oklahoma town. She was old and not very mobile when she left Aunt Bess' and moved out to the Confederate home. By that time we were speaking. It was a great tragedy that made her relent and speak to us. My sister Mary and her husband were involved in an accident in Utah when they were with Aunt Bess's daughter and her husband, driving to California. Max, the husband was killed and the rest severely injured. This news was 'wirelessed' to Aunt Bess and Aunt Meg came across the street to tell us. In the face of the sudden, sad news, Meg and mother threw their arms around each other – and it was as if they had been friends all their lives.

Young Elisabeth

I was the youngest of eight but, by the time I came along, the older ones were married and away from home. Two of my sisters lived in our town and I used to go over and spend the day with them. How much I learned, as Mary would give me a bushel of Alberta peaches to skin and pack in jars while she made the syrup for canning. Mildred would let me help sew clothes for her two little girls.

My passion was for animals. There was always a cat and a dog of my own, although Papa did not approve of animals that didn't work for their living. I acquired Frances Scott Layfollotte Galt when I was in the third grade. A pal had brought an old leather satchel to school with four pups which she proceeded to hand out to anyone who wanted one. Her mother had warned her not to come home with them again as she and the mother dog were both tired of minding them. In history we were learning about explorers and by the time I got home Frances had been christened. She was a mongrel fox terrier; she was very sleek and inviting to the opposite sex. It wasn't long before she was pregnant, and papa said I could keep her only if I had her 'fixed' after her first litter of pups. By this time, there was a Vet in our town and he offered to do the necessary for five dollars; a princely sum which my brother and I had to find. However, there were so many pups in the litter we sold them handsomely with the net result of ten dollars. This paid for the operation and enough money to have as many banana splits as we could eat for a long time to come.

When I was about ten my father was busy building the first proper road through the Arbuckle mountains, the range of jagged mountains that runs through the southern part of Oklahoma. It was such a hot summer that he decided that he would move the family out to the camp in the mountains where it would be cooler, and they could swim in the mountain stream and pools.

The road was being built by convict labour, because there was very little other labour available. The gang was in striped uniform, but they were free to go about their work unshackled, under the eye of an armed guard. It was tough work, hacking roads out of solid rock, quarrying their own stone and even surviving in that petrifying Oklahoma summer heat. Rattlesnakes abounded in the mountains, and one had to be ready for emergencies. If a man was bitten by a snake there were two things to do, burn the bite out or cut it out with a knife. There was one time when no fire or knife was available, and to save a man's life my father soused his mouth out with whiskey, then bit away the snake bite. I never relished his telling that story.

With us that summer we had Frances, who soon got to realise that when the men shouted "Fire in the Hole" you were supposed to run and hide under a bed. The men would put the dynamite into the holes, shout the "Fire in the Hole", press the charge and the rock face of the mountains would fall away with a terrific roll of thunder. Old Frances to her dying day would hide under a bed if anyone shouted "Fire in the Hole".

When I was about twelve Mother had to have a womanly operation and it was done at the Hardy Sanatorium one block away. Her room was on the second floor, just by a metal fire escape. All went well, but Mother was bored without all the animals at home. One day she asked if I would bring Frances to see her and explained to me I could sneak her up the fire escape in the middle of the morning when things were quiet. Laboriously, I carried Frances up the high, steep fire escape and cautiously opened the door to Mother's room. Mother pulled back the covers and motioned me to put Frances under the covers. I don't think either one of us thought of germs, dogs in bed and regulations. Just at that moment the matron came in on a tour of inspection. Both daughter and dog were barred from visiting Mother for the rest of her stay. As she grew old Frances became over-indulgent in food and with such short legs, under-indulgent in exercise. Soon she grew a heavy undercarriage that she almost had to hoist when she went over the street curbs.

The town that I lived in really shouldn't be in existence today, but it was like the proverbial cat with nine lives. It couldn't be killed. When I was in the third grade (or third form) a tornado struck the town and razed it to the ground. The tornadoes started in the Gulf of Mexico, gained speed across the wide plains of Texas and usually hit in Oklahoma. There was literally no warning of these until the engine driver on the one railroad through the town thought out an idea. If, as he was speeding across the plains, he saw the cone-like funnel of a tornado he hung on to his train whistle for all he was worth, and the little towns that he went through could take warning. One morning at school, we heard the dreaded prolonged, shrieking note of the whistle. Our teacher thought perhaps it would be a false alarm and didn't take us to the storm cellar, but rather put us in the north side of the building, for the tornado if it came, would be coming from the south. She then put us to singing hymns, but through our unnatural singing there came a deadly silence followed by a terrific thud, and the building shook with an awful blast. When the teacher opened the door of the classroom to let us out, there was nothing left but the room in which we were - the rest of the building had been cut clean off.

By this time, it was becoming a promising industry in the state. Our town was the residential town lying some eighteen miles from the nearest oil town. The word would come that a gusher was due, and the whole town would turn out to see the well come in. The frantic workings of the men to be ready when she arrived, the sudden billowing and the huge gusher of oil that sprayed through the derrick, high up into the air drenching all in greasy, gold garnering oil. If this caught fire it was indeed a spectacle.

The oil was then piped from the wells to the oil tankards lying on the railroad in our town. Great precaution had to be taken against smoking when these were being filled. Men sat on the tankards, holding the pipeline into the opening of the tank, until it was full, then quickly capping it. But one lazy day, one man who had already filled his tank, closed his cap, sat upon it and against regulation lit a pipe, tossing his match into the air. The gust of wind carried it by accident into the opening of the next tank. The explosion that resulted is long remembered, and that year is referred to as the year of the explosion. The town was almost completely wrecked.

Then there were dust storms which were far from pleasant. You would wake to a bright, beautiful morning, and suddenly it would grow dark, with the thick darkness of an eerie fog. If you were in the house you raced to all the windows and jammed them down tight. If you were out, you somehow managed to wet your handkerchief and tie it over your face -only just in time as the wind swept clouds of dust from off the plains and it swelled and enveloped all the buildings, blotting out every sign of humanity. The thick dust reigned supreme, and when it gradually grew lighter, the choking and burning in your throat sopped, and you were able to see about you again. Inside the house was as if someone had sprayed a good layer of fine dust over all the furniture and carpets. Outside, your heart cried out for rain to come and wash away the brown covering that made everything the same hues. No green, no flowers, no shrubs - only dust, dust, dust.

The second loan Papa had from the bank came about because oil had been discovered to the North, East, South and West of our large ranch about twenty miles outside of town. Papa concluded that, if it was on all sides it was bound to be in the middle as well. I don't think he bothered about a geologist and tests, he just went to his friend, the bank Manager, and borrowed another twenty thousand to pay for the rigging, drilling and discovery of oil. It was a dry hole, no oil at all – but we were the only kids in our grade who had an oil derrick to play on. I don't think Papa ever made any money from the ranch but he did enjoy all the activities there. There were cherry groves and he had a saw mill whose mighty efforts yielded the wood for our subsequent cherry dining room suite. There was a sorghum mill, which made sweet smelling molasses. There was cotton, corn, pecan groves, pigs and cattle – which meant plenty of rabbits and squirrels for shooting. Papa used to take me out to the ranch in the buggy when I was very little. About ten or twelve, he decided I should learn how to shoot a shotgun. He put old tin cans on the fence posts and taught me the rudiments of how to knock them off. It was my shoulder I almost knocked off instead.

To Mama I was her precious daughter who had to be protected from the dangers of this world. I couldn't understand this because nothing phased me. Mother was especially scared of water and drowning, and when I asked if I could go to the Store and see if they had a bathing suit so I could join the rest of the 'gang' learning how to swim at Blue Hole – she told me No, I wasn't to go near the water. A friend had been given a yard of bright red calico to make dolls clothes. I thought it would make a splendid bathing suit and offered her a nickel for it. She quickly accepted the offer and I secreted the red calico home, cut out a bathing suit and stitched it up by hand, being very proud of my efforts. Before I had a chance to try it out a Blue Hole, a torrential rain came and all the streets were running with cascading water down the side gulley's. The gang donned their bathing attire and went out to play in the heaven-sent water. I went proudly out in my red calico. It must have been a very cheap calico for the red dye wasn't set and soon my body became that of a red Indian. Mother was so embarrassed at the sight of her daughter that she marched me to the store and bought me a bathing suit; this was something that she could ill afford.

A Bit Personal – background, article from the Daily Ardmoreite
c. April 1930

Notes of interest concerning folk you know gathered here and there by members of the staff of the Daily Ardmorette.

You may not believe in what is called the science of numerology or astrology but here is a succession of events that will make you wonder. Lee L. Galt is always apprehensive when April 16 comes. When his daughter, Miss Mildred, who is now Mrs Cecil Baber, was brought home from school with a broken arm on April 16 he was pale with fear in remembering the sad things which this day in previous years had brought him.

It was April 16, 1876, he left Georgia for Texas; it was on April 16, 1877, when he received deep burns upon his body in an accident; the scars remain today; it was April 16, 1878, when he received severe gunshot wounds, the scars of which mar his body today; it was April 16, 1896, when he lost his first wife; it was April 16, 1902, when he lost his second wife. They were both Georgia women and their bodies are in Rose Hill cemetery. It was April 16, 1907, when the daughter was brought from school suffering from a broken arm. It was April 16, 1928 that his house was burned and he lost all his personal effects.

But despite this series of coincidents which have brought grief and suffering and loss, Lee L. Galt has left more tracks in Ardmore than any other one man. He was the contractor on the oil mill in 1893. The construction work was of stone. He built the two viaducts across the railroad tracks in the north-east section of the city.

He built an aqueduct under the Santa Fe near union depot. He built Rod and Gun Club Lake in 1896. He built the Winsor hotel which used to stand in the unit block of North Washington. It was of stone construction. The Love building on East Main Street destroyed in the 1915 explosion was another of his buildings. The Kloski Opera house that stood just east of the Whittington hotel was another building erected by him. The Tyler & Simpson Company building is another foot print of his.

About the biggest contract he ever undertook was to make and deliver to the Santa Fe railway company over 200,000 crossties. The company turned down something like 100,000 of the ties and broke him. The City National bank was on his bond and to save them he sold his home and his teams and whatever property he had accumulated and started all over again. The bank did not pay out one penny for him.

When statehood was conferred upon Oklahoma the roads were not located upon section lines in the Indian Territory section of the state. The huge jobs of opening roads on section lines lay with each county. Carter county met that emergency by employing Lee L. Galt for the job. He was given charge of the county prisoners and a crew of surveyors and roads were marked and opened and improved. This required six steady years of work.

His first move from Georgia was to Minneola, Texas and from Minneola he came to Ardmore in 1889. He was the first Galt to move here. His first business venture was to buy out J. F. Ridenour who owned and operated the Ardmore Transfer company. He took over the teams and wagons and did team contracting until losses caused him to sell his business.

Other members of the Galt family were John L. Galt, Wilborn J. Galt, known as Buddy Galt, James E. Galt, Mrs Margaret O. Giddens, Mrs Bessie M. Smith and Mrs Mary Sewell. All the sons in the family are dead except Lee but two daughters survive and live in Ardmore.

The children of Lee L. Galt are Mrs Machen Johnson, Oklahoma City; Mrs Lucius N. Cox, Ardmore; Mrs Cecil Baber, Ardmore; Miss Elisabeth Galt, Ardmore; John O Galt, Santa Rosa, Texas; Leland L. Galt Jr, Grand Rapids, Mich; and Monroe S. Galt, Ardmore.

Mr Galt's third wife is also a Georgia woman. They were married in 1905 and live at the Cedars in south-west Ardmore. He is a member of the Masonic fraternity and is a Knight Templar and is also a member of the First Baptist church.

Miss Margaret O. Giddens, sister, who was possessed of a very bright mind and with a fine memory, was a teacher in her younger days and the Georgia Galt family all except John, the oldest, was educated by her.

The last achievement of Mr Galt's in the way of construction work was to direct the clearing and ditching and draining and terracing of the Bear Creek farms, a tract of 880 acres in the northwest section of Carter county.

Chapter Two
Anglicized At Last

When I was ten years old I had a cat, that I called Sir Thomas. "But why call it Sir Thomas, when it lives in the wilds of Oklahoma," friends asked.
"I don't know. It feels like a Sir Thomas to me." I replied.
I often wonder if that was my unconscious inkling that in later life I would have more than a cat that claimed to be English.
Sir Thomas grew up, lived happily and died English in name only. I grew up, lived happily, English by marriage - over twenty one years of it. I now assume that I have become of age as an Englishwoman.
It's a long jaunt from Oklahoma to England, so I shall begin at the beginning. In the then wilds of Oklahoma (it had only been a state two years when I was born) I grew tall and strong like the corn. As my legs grew, so did my brain, and I stretched out for further fields at the University of Chicago. At the age of twenty I was back in Oklahoma, teaching in the same high school from which I had graduated. Some of the students in the class were as big as I was and almost as old -- -- but we ignored the similarities and buried ourselves in Latin and French.
At the end of two years teaching I had saved enough money to 'do' Europe. I joined the proverbial tour, saw the proverbial sights 'oh-ed and ah-ed' over all things quaint in England, then neatly put all the details and experiences in a mental packet and shelved it as 'To Be Perused Later'.
At the end of my third year teaching I had saved enough to have a year off and acquire another degree. This time I went to Columbia University in New York City and lived at International House on Riverside Drive.
As one of the new lot of females at International House, I was duly given the once over by male members of the previous year. One Englishman's gaze seemed to linger. When he began to talk about 'roses round the cottage door', I decided it was time to think seriously

about England. As fate would have it, I fell very ill with a mastoid and meningitis two weeks after we were engaged. It was then that I knew that it was England for me definitely. If he could love me through anaesthetics, bandaged head, and deathly weakness - it was the real thing.

We had to wait a year for me to pull my socks up physically, and for him to finish his Doctor's Degree. Being English: hence cautious and deliberate by nature, he wanted to make sure that I knew what I was letting myself in for by coming to live in England. According to him, the England that I had seen previously was the England shown to American tourists: London, Stratford, Windsor, Oxford, Cambridge and the Lakes. He wanted me to see the England in which I was going to live. We came over the summer before we were married, letting the sea breezes heal my recuperating body and the land breezes reveal the future lay-out.

His Mother and Father met us at the boat in Liverpool. Mother B. was waving a white scarf as she stood on the quay, surrendering before she had ever met me. Dear Mother B.! I was the opposite of everything that she had hoped for in a daughter-in-law. I was American instead of English; I had University degrees (these might spoil my chances at being a contented wife and mother); I came from Oklahoma (which heretofore in her knowledge had produced only cowboys and Indians); I used lip-stick, wore ear-rings, and worst of all - I smoked. But she had great faith in God and her son, and she accepted me dutifully into her home. As the years passed her duty changed to love, and I knew that I was finally accepted when she asked me - years later, to open her village's Mothers Union Fair.

Father B. was a different proposition. Any American daughter-in-law wasn't a challenge but a delight to him. He used to buy cigarettes for me, inveigle me into the garage to look at his fish-rods and flies, where I could smoke in peace.
It was a wonder that that exploratory try was a success. We met so many Waterloos! - mainly over the simple use of words. The second morning at Mother B's was almost disastrous. It was summer and the windows were wide open. The previous night before going to sleep, I had read in bed, bothered somewhat by the little gnats that came in through the open window by the light. At breakfast Mother B. asked if I had slept well the night before.

"Yes, after I had killed all the bugs in my bed, " I replied. She rose in one mighty swoop of temper.

"I'll have you know that there are, and never have been, any bugs in my house," she said.

It took an hour's explanation on the part of her son (who did want to marry this American) to convince his Mother that in America anything that flies is called a bug. In a few precise words he informed me that bugs were never found, and certainly never mentioned, in polite society in England.

It was the same in London, when meeting his relatives. The day was very hot, so I asked after tea,

"Auntie, do you think I could put on my bathing suit and go into your backyard and sunbathe?"

She, too, rose in one majestic swoop and exclaimed,

"I'll have you know Uncle has spent hundreds of pounds and hours of loving work on what you call a backyard." It wasn't till we had lived in Glasgow that I truly felt what Auntie meant when she said backyard.

After a three week, weakening tour, we sailed from Liverpool to New York and motored from there to Oklahoma. The mad Englishman was presented on the spot and won the heart of every Isolationist there.

The following year we were married in the Lady Chapel of the Cathedral of St. John the Divine in New York City. The echoes of the groom's "I do" still reverberate in the dome. His English room-mates had made him practice so successfully to get the right intonation and volume to suit an American service, that he put his whole power into it. The guests quivered. I quaked, then got the giggles, and we were off to a laughing start.

After three hectic weeks honeymooning in New York, seeing twenty-one shows - we sailed for England, married and secure. Our only salvation was that we knew each other's country and presumable background. Also we were armed with a sense of humour. True the English and American sense of humour are very different - the means, not the end, that is.

We set up our new abode in the Northeast coast of England, where my husband was in private practice and also lecturing at the University. He was very busy so handed over the job of furnishing our house to me.

"But what do we need?" I asked.

"You know! A lounge suite, a dining room suite, a bedroom suite ----" I went into Newcastle to a large furnishing store with my very long list and set to work. That evening I was duly asked,

"And how did you get on with the furniture?"

"Fine," I answered. "Everything ordered, suite by suite."

"In the dining room suite how many chairs did it include?"

"Four," I answered. "Why?"

"Do you think that will be enough. It is quite possible that someday we may have children, and if we should have guests at the same time, we'll need more chairs. You had better order another two."

Next day I dutifully traipsed into the same Newcastle shop and asked to see the young man who had waited on me yesterday.

The young lady looked around the store and said,

"I see no one waiting here. Are you sure you are supposed to meet him here? There is a telephone around the corner if you would like to phone and make certain."

I tried to explain with increasing noise and gibberish until I finally succeeded in arousing the young man who had waited on me the previous day. He came out of the office to find out if he could help.

"Oh, there he is," I cried.

"Why, he hasn't been waiting on you. He has been here all the time," the young lady volunteered. To wait on, or to serve, does it matter?

In due course I realised that I was pregnant and being so new to the country, embarrassed and scared around all Englishmen except one ---- I wanted a woman doctor. I got out the telephone book, and looked through all the A's, but there was no woman doctor. Under the B's there were none, but under the C's there was a Dr. Mabel Campbell. It was a miracle of discovery; she took me to her capable bosom with open arms. If I were ill and she came visiting me, she was always accompanied by her devoted spaniel, Caesar, who invariably christened whatever curtains happened to be hanging near.

"You must forgive him; he's very much a Caesar," she would say.

When our son was born Dr. Mabel presented him with a layette that she had knitted in between giving lectures at the University. She was to have delivered our second baby, but unfortunately fell and broke her neck two weeks before the baby was due. Dr. Mabel had been visiting a poor patient and fell down her narrow dark stairs. Her new assistant made the delivery of my daughter, but for the post-natal check-up I went to her surgery. I was ushered into Dr. Mabel's bedroom where she was sitting up in bed massaging the feeble arm of a young boy patient. Her hated dog-collar for her broken neck was lying on the floor. She insisted upon living for others when there was so little life in her. Three months later she was dead, but so strong was her impact upon me that to me she still lives.

When our daughter was nine months old war was declared. We had become good friends with the American consul in Newcastle, who phoned and said that he was holding three places on a ship, taking evacuees to the States. According to him, I owed it to my children to take them out of harm's way. According to me, I owed it to my husband to stay. I had married him for better or for worse - hence his country for better or for worse, and I shouldn't go running home to Mama when danger threatened. I refused his kind offer and said that I would brave the war out in England. It was as if I had had God's blessing on my decision. The ship on which I had decided not to travel, was the Athenia, lost with so many Mothers and children 'escaping from war'.

The first nine months of the phoney war soon settled into routine. As we were on the N.E. Coast between two big rivers which had barrage balloon protection, every enemy aircraft would zoom in and out, casting any unused bombs on our village. The nightly routine consisted of siren sounding, piling the two children into the pram with covers, thermos and biscuits - then plunking Dinah, the family pug, on top. We would then race for the village communal shelter, built on the edge of our front garden.

This nightly diversion palled when a land mine destroyed the house behind us and fifty small bombs pitted the field adjoining. We decided we should take the children away from the coast. We found an excellent little cottage in Otterburn and established ourselves with the children, animals and nurse maid (not yet called up as she was under eighteen). Neatly settled in for two weeks, we had to pull up roots and move as the R.A.M.C. had commandeered our cottage for nurses who would supply the nearby hospital.

Again we sought refuge inland and found an old house in Hexham which claimed both a ghost and the possibility of evacuees being billeted upon the occupier. The ghost, an escapee from the Battle of Hexham years ago, we never saw. As for the evacuees, two twelve year old girls, we took them to our hearts. To supplement the meat ration, we bred rabbits for food, only to find that all of us hated the taste of rabbits and not one of us could bring himself to kill one. For vegetables, I dug and managed two allotments myself.

My husband, rejected by the army because of a bad knee, went into the Ministry of Labour. To pull my war weight, other than the house, the children, the animals, the hens, the rabbits, and the allotments - I went periodically into Newcastle to give blood transfusions, and I helped run the library in the big military hospital in Hexham.

In one big ward of this hospital, I became very friendly with a sea captain who had been on the bridge of his ship when it received a direct hit. Part of his hip had been blown away and the wound would not heal. One Tuesday, he told me that on the following Friday he was going to have a 'do or die' operation. I wished him the best of luck.

On that Friday I had been busy digging at the allotment for three hours and came home tired and dirty. The phone rang. It was the hospital, saying they had been on to the blood bank in Newcastle for some special blood, and found that I ---- as a donor ---- lived on the spot. Could I come at once as a man's life depended on it after an operation. I asked if I had time for a bath as I was very dirty after digging. "No! Come at once!"

I mounted my bike and sailed the two downhill miles to the hospital, to be greeted by blood spattered nurses and doctors who took me straight into the operation theatre and tapped me. When it was all over, I asked if the name of the patient was Captain X of Ward Y.
"Yes, it is. Do you know him?" I explained about my visits to the wards.

The following Tuesday when I went on my library rounds, I went into the Captain's. His bed was at the far end, but the minute I stepped into the door I could feel his eyes, drawing me to his bedside.
"Hello, how are you today? It looks as if it were a 'do' and not a 'die', I said as he beamed upon me.

"Yes," he replied "and I hear that it was you who gave me the most needed blood."

"It was nothing," I answered.

"Indeed, it was," he returned. "You see, not only did you save me life, but I've always wanted a drop of Yankee blood. Now I have it."

From Hexham my husband was called to London to work on a post-war training scheme (already they were planning for after the war when they hadn't even finished it, let alone win it.) He went ahead and I sold the house, packed up, and started on the journey to London. It was a nightmare of a journey with lots of raids which meant that the train was sided: two children, wildly excited and a young nursemaid who was making her first long train journey. But above all in my care was one very pregnant dog. I had muzzled her as required and taken her along to the guard's van. He took one look at her expanded sides and said,

"Madam, the responsibility is yours and the bitch's. You hold her all the way to London."

But she was a clever bitch; she held her puppies until we reached our London home that night. Then she produced a litter of eight, elegant pups. These pups proved to be a heaven-sent diversion for all of us in those early days in London, when buzz bombs had replaced ordinary bombs, and life was very extra-ordinary.

We kept all eight pups. Since any pups were very scarce a shop in Bake Street said that they would consider buying the litter even if they were cross-bred. I was to bring a sample of the pups down when they were eight weeks old. Since the journey was a long one and I knew the shop couldn't resist the pups once they had seen them, we took the whole litter in. I gave each child one in each hand, and the same for the nursemaid and myself. We boarded the bus into town; a retinue of pups.

To my horror when we reached the shop, there was a fine litter of highly bred pups in the window. The shop owner would not even look at my litter of mongrels. Dejected, we four and the eight pups trouped out of the shop and approached the nearest policeman. I asked if he knew any shop that would buy them.

"There is one in Camden Town, which prides itself on buying anything from a snake to an elephant. Your pups should be somewhere in between."

We piled on another bus, reached Camden Town and ferreted out the Pet Shop. Yes, the man would buy them. That is - the dogs. He would take the bitches off my hands for nothing. This offer bore out my theory on the role of females in this world, but I let him take all eight. Food to feed them on was so scarce that I could not argue.

The war days passed quickly studded with incidents in the mere act of surviving. One night one of my husband's aunts was having supper with us, and as a special treat I made waffles. The iron was sizzling on the table when we heard a buzz bomb creeping near. As we had ignored the previous warning, and the waffles smelled so good, we decided not to go into the garden shelter but to use the heavy dining table as protection. We transferred the family and the waffles underneath - all except Auntie. Getting her under was quite a problem as she had arthritis and couldn't bend. We had her lie flat on her back and we heaved her under. To the accompaniment of much noise outside, we devoured the waffles. It was another problem getting Auntie out when the raid was over.

That Christmas we phoned the American Red Cross and asked if they knew of two American soldiers who would like family hospitality for the day. Two enormous sergeants arrived. We were much taken with them, and amazed that neither was married; as it was, two girls were missing golden opportunities.

"Why have I never married," queried one of them. "Well, it's like this. The girl I marry must have red hair and must be able to play the organ. Up to date I have not found a red-headed organist.

The daily game of the children was to collect shrapnel from the raid of the night before. It was only recently that I came across the heavy box, nursing its weighty collection. They seemed such harmless bits now.

Domestic developments were occurring: my son's school had been hit during a raid and was closed; my husband secured another job, this time in Glasgow. We decided to send the children on to their grandparents near Buxton, while we packed up. Auntie said she would take them on the train as she wanted a breathing space from the raids. A few days before they were due to leave, I was cycling home from shopping and passed a badly hit block of houses with no sign of human habitation. My cycle swerved as it struck something, and a poor tortoise deserted by its owners looked up blankly at me. His head wagged as if to say, "So glad you ran into me." I reached down and stroked his head which he made no effort to retract. I popped him into my cycle basket and made for home.

He was duly christened Oscar and a small travelling cage was built for him to accompany the children. On the day we were to meet Auntie at the station in town, the children, I and Oscar in his new cage set off across the Heath to catch the bus. Three times we had to throw ourselves under hedges as 'things came near'. We reached the station, bedraggled and dirty - still with Oscar, when another siren went. We could hear it overhead, but no one in the train queue moved or wavered. All eyes were focussed on a little girl and boy clutching a tortoise in a cage.

In Glasgow we lived high on a hill in an established suburb. The view was commanding, the houses majestic, and we soon came to find colour in what we first thought was only greyness.

The language problem rose its awkward head again. One day there was a knock on the front door. I answered and there was a portly minister.

"Please, could I speak to Miss Anderson who lives here."

"I'm sorry" I replied. "She has been dead several months." We had bought the house from her estate.

"Indeed, I'm grieved to hear that. Could I send a message up to her then?" If anybody could, I thought he would have been able to. I tried again.

"You don't understand. She passed away three months ago."

"Oh dear! I thought you said she had been in bed for three months."

I soon became very glad that we had come to Scotland. I came to know and love the Scots, when before I had thought them very hard to know. It takes time, but when you are accepted, they give you their hearts.

After our first year there war ended and peace descended. The chance of a maid came my way again. She was a great success, Mary, who came from the Gorbals and had never been in service before. She arrived, clutching her worldly possessions in a brown paper parcel. She had never known a bathroom before, but once initiated became the best bathed person in Glasgow.

She didn't know what saucers were for and the first time she was asked to set the tea table, put cups minus saucers. It was this appalling ignorance that made her so easy to teach. She soon became the proverbial treasure. There was no crime, filth or degradation that Mary did not know first-hand. One brother was in Borstal, the father was frequently 'had up' for beating the mother, and a sister married the week before her baby was due. Yet she, herself, had a rigid sense of self-discipline, as long as she was with us. When she returned home for her days off, she reverted to her old self. She maintained that she had to, as her family teased her for being 'posh' if she didn't.

After four years in Glasgow, during which time the children developed warm Scottish accents, we found ourselves on the verge of moving to England again. Just before our leaving, we were attending the Royal Garden Party at Holyrood Palace. A casual business friend spotted my husband and came up.

"I hear you're leaving Scotland. You will hate to leave Edinburgh, won't you?"

"But it isn't Edinburgh we live. It's Glasgow," we replied.

"Then you won't hate leaving that at all!"

But we did! The rivalry of the two cities meant nothing to us, when our hearts were left behind in Glasgow.

Embedded again in England with no war to worry us out of our beds - or our minds - the children have grown up. They go home periodically with me to pay love and respects to the American family, but however hard they are urged to stay and make it their home, they are eager to get back to England. The same with me. I suddenly look about me, sniff the moist, soothing English air - no dust storms and no tornadoes - and I suddenly realize that I am Anglicized at last. I no longer ever feel cold, I love the gracious rain, I prefer roast beef to fried chicken, I understand all my husband's jokes and I would like to retire in the Cotswolds not California.

Chapter 3
The Letters

My Mother was christened Rowena Elizabeth Galt after her Mother, Rowena. She was called Elizabeth during her childhood in Oklahoma but changed the spelling when she married and moved to England- she signed all the letters sent to her parents during the war as Elisabeth. After she moved to Liverpool in 1949 she called herself Betty (Bradbury) and that is what our family called her. Later when she came to live with the Newton Family at the White House , she was known as Granny to all and sundry.

My Mother wrote to her parents;

**Mr and Mrs Lee Galt ,
125 Stanley Boulevard,
Ardmore
Oklahoma,
USA.**

The Letters were very small- 13 cm x 8 ½ cm, with 2 ½ pence of stamps on.
Some 5 x ½ p green stamps and some 2 ½ blue stamps .
Some letters had been opened by an examiner, and had a label saying - Opened by Examiner 5291.
Some were type written on thin airmail paper and some hand written on thicker paper

**Lee and Rowena Galt
Ardmore**

She always put on the back of the envelope, hand written- From their daughter – Mrs. R. Bradbury, and the address where she was living at that time. They span from 26th February 1940 to 16th November 1945 covering life in the UK during The Second World War.

Some were short and some were long, all telling the day to day happenings in the Bradbury household, especially how my brother Lee and I were doing.
All written in positive and upbeat mode, no complaints and no misgivings about her life, despite being in a country at war.

It is implied that my Mother tried to write once a week to her mother in America. The letters had to travel about 5000 miles, across the Atlantic by ship and then by train across America to Oklahoma- mid west. The letters are printed as they were written – some of the language may be deemed offensive today.

My American grandmother who I only met twice – on a visit to America in 1946 and another in 1954, kept all the letters my mother had sent to her, and then sent them to me in the early 60's – for which I am forever grateful. Being older now and slightly wiser, I have realised the importance of these documents, not only to our family history but as an intimate record of life in wartime Britain.

Sue Newton

World War II - Timeline

1st September 1939 - Hiltler invades Poland.

3rd September 1939 - Britain and France declare war on Germany

6th June 1944 - D Day - Allied invasion of France

7th May 1945 - Germany Surrenders.

The Letters

The variety of typed and hand written letters and stamps sent from the UK to Ardmore, Oklahoma during the war.

List of houses that the Bradbury Family lived in during the War

1940 - Ardmore , South Shields, Northumberland ,England . Ronald had designed this house himself, and named it Ardmore for his American wife.Ronald was unfit for the forces but was working for the Ministry of Labour in the North East

1941 - Holly House, Quatre Bras, Hexham, Northumberland. Ronald moved the family out of Newcastle on Tyne because of enemy action at the coast and they evacuated to Hexham, living in rented property .

1943 - 8 Thornton Way, London, NW 11.Ronald was asked to go to work in London, he wanted to have the family stay safe up in the Northumberland country side, but Elisabeth insisted all the family should remain together, so they all moved down to London, in the middle of all the bombing.

1944 - Moray Lodge, 25 Newark Drive , Pollokshields, Glasgow, Scotland .Ronald was made Director of Housing for Glasgow by the government, to begin the task of rebuilding the City when the war was over, so all the family moved up to Scotland.

1949 - After the war Ronald applied and became City Architect and Director of Housing for Liverpool . The family moved to the White House , Grassendale Park, Liverpool 19.

Letter One

Ardmore
February 26th, 1940

Dear Mother and Papa,

Another week peacefully passed, ushered in by strangest of things – none other than spring itself. It is so delightful to see the green grass, the shrubs and paths minus their coat of snow. It was almost as if we lived in Iceland we had so much snow and ice. However a rapid thaw cleared it all away, mild sunshiny days greet us each morning. Daylight Saving Time has been introduced again so with the extra hour and spring itself we all feel remade.

Lee and Susan are again allowed to play out and romp around the garden as they see fit. It's an old life for Lee and he has resumed his old games and outside toys. He has a garage for his new toys outside and a proper garage man he is, the way he park his car, his trike, his bicycle, scooter, wagon and sand toys. As for Susan, here so far she's been allowed out in the garden only installed in her pram, where she spent hours watching the cars go by and greeting all the stray dogs who stopped to pay their respects. But she is on her feet – clothed in an old legging suit of Lee's and his first wellingtons. What a time she has. She dashes about like a middle-aged busy body who doesn't have time to stop and think. At first she couldn't manage all the ups and downs, rockeries, etc. – but now she has become brave and toddles on and on. She's a terror for putting things in her mouth to sample them' and has tasted sand, twigs and stones – but you can trust her to spit them out eventually, so we just let her roam. Today she spent a long time chasing Donald, our big white duck which Ronald claims 'is the world's most colossal duck'.

Another brightening feature of the week is Ronald's recovery, his freedom from isolation and his return to work. He has had a 'do' (as the Sheilds people say) but seems recovered and much more rested. Tonight he is hard at work setting exam questions for the Easter Finals. The firm is getting in new work which is unusual in this war time business when most building has ceased. One of his most recent schools appeared in the last issue of Architect's journal and it made a splendid show.

England seems more cheerful in regard to the war. Mr Well's visit to Europe is hailed as a good sign. Poor Finland – we do feel sorry for her – she had such a gallant struggle. As for local activity there has been none inland but quite a bit off the coast when our fighters chase off attacking bombers from the fishing fleets. The price of fish has soared enormously because of the danger accompanying the getting of it. However we again seem to offering better protection there – and the price has gone down accordingly.

I am making new marmalade this week. The Seville oranges have been plentiful but sugar is limited to 3lbs per person in the household – to be used for marmalade (you see what a breakfast institution English Marmalade is) which means that we got 15lbs. In order to get this I had to take the receipt for my oranges to the local Food Control office which gave me a permit to buy the said 15lbs from the grocer with whom I am registered. I think the grocers are about brainless with their extra book keeping and coupon clipping.

Did I tell you we are contemplating keeping chickens? Their price for eggs is amazing now and it is remembered that in the last war it went up to 6d (12c) each. Since we use so many we thought it would be guaranteed if we keep our own chickens. Their feed will be difficult to get but they say we will always be able to get some sort – and then too we can augment it by scraps and peelings. We are buying a proper chicken house – and six pullets now and six in September.

Lee and I helped Ramsey, the gardener on Saturday – the first day the latter was able to work due to frozen ground. England's slogan is Dig for Victory so that most of our produce can be grown at home. We, as well as many of our neighbours are filling our flower beds with carrots, turnips etc. in order to leave our vegetable gardens for potatoes, peas, etc. It's going to be fun to see just what and how much we can produce. Lee's going to have his own special plot – let's hope he works magic with it.

All of the goldfish in the pond were killed by the long freeze – so Lee and two friends of his planned a funeral for this afternoon, but they were beaten by the seagulls who spied them first. As a result there were only two left to bury, and these were dutifully turned over to Patrick Michael for rituals.

Susan just woke up (9 o'clock) and I brought her down for a chat but now she has gone back again. She's cutting an eye tooth (which she overlooked and jumped to a back molar before) and seems a bit excited. She's very good with her sleeping and it's only in the last few days that she hasn't had both an afternoon and morning nap. And she sleeps till nine in the morning.

We have had no further news from you since the second combined one. We both hope that Papa has continued to improve under Mother's loving care. It's a long job – I know but everything worthwhile is. Keep your spirits high and you'll get better twice as fast. May our distant thoughts and close love help you. Keep happy – both of you.

Love and kisses from us all,

Your,
Elisabeth.

Dear Mother and Father,

You will have gathered from the bright tone of Betty's letters to you that England in wartime is not nearly as bad a place as we expected it to be. So far life, apart from some very minor discomforts, is very much the same. So don't worry at all about the Bradbury family. We are all thriving. You can rest assured that we will give you an entirely honest picture of conditions here. With love to you both,

Your loving son,
Ronald.

Elisabeth, with Lee and Susan in Ardmore.

Letter Two

Ardmore
Mar 7, 1940

To Mr. and Mrs. Lee Galt
125 Stanley Blvd.
Ardmore, Oklahoma, USA

Dear Mother and Papa

So far this week there is no further report from you, so I take it as read that Papa is steadily improving and Mother is happy and pleased with his progress. We enjoyed last week's letter giving Papa's own version of the accident. Isn't it nice to look back on it as a thing of the past?
I wish I could say that Ronald's boils were a thing of the past – but they are giving him a wretched time. No sooner do some get over than others appear. Two monsters on his left arm are rendering it useless and very painful. The Doctor has at last changed his injection treatment and we are hoping for better results soon. He's at work again – and doing very well to be up and about.
There is little of news to report – except a new eye tooth from Susan and the joy of living in both her and Lee. She looks forward each afternoon to our long walk to get her from school. Dinah usually goes with us but as she's very much a Lady at present we have to leave her at home. Lee tells his pals, when they ask where Dinah is - "Oh, she's got the measles!"

I've been working quite a lot in the garden these days now they are bright and springlike. Our sunken pond was outrageously flooded because of the too-much ice and snow and I've spent all day pumping and bucketing it out. I thought how Mother used to consider it a spring job. Also, I've given all the lawns a dose of bone meal and sand. Ramsey, the gardener, comes all day on each Saturday – and we confer as to what my week's work should be. I feel like a Head Girl with all my garden activity.
Ronald has bought a chicken house which should be in function in about a week. Lee's looking forward to having chickens and promises he will look after them.
He was greatly puzzled the other day because he couldn't understand how the enemy had put coal mines in the sea and our ships hit them. A mine was a mine to him. He has two week's holiday at Easter – and as Ronald has a

month from College, he's going to try to get off from the office and we're planning to go to a farm near Allendale – a small beautiful village away in the hills. People are always taking farm holidays in England – as they are so novel to the usual run of life – and of course now they are twice cherished because they are in safe zones – presumably. We are all looking forward to two weeks there – and the change and rest should make Ronald a new man. I hope so for his sake. Will you two join us? I know you would be interested in our English farm holiday.

Susan, when we take her out now, almost breaks her reins which hold her in her pram – to be down and about. She can push her pram about two or three blocks. If you'll let her. Her eyes are the brightest blue-purple and show no signs of changing. However her hair is darkening and growing very thick although no curl is enticed there as yet. Her cheeks are full and rosy – and the twinkle in her eye is no body's business. In fact – how I wish you could see her.

Lee's school is putting on a children's play. His version of it caused such laughter on Ronald's part, he had to stop because Lee thought we were laughing at him. However – as Lee says "I'm to be an Imp. I have to freeze – but not really freeze – things and people, by pretending to throw – but not really throw – frost at them! He's so much of a Imp anyway – it seems a good role for him.

This seems to exhaust what little news there is, so I'll say a fond goodnight and hope you both are well and happy – for we are. Never worry about us – life is good and life is full – it's all in the way you look at it.

All our love and kisses

Your,
Elisabeth

Lee and Susan.

Letter Three

Holly House
July 6, 1941

Dear Mother and Papa:

This week's letter from you brought the sad and unfortunate news of Monroe's accident. I am so sorry and do hope that by now the arm and shoulder are out of the cast and that massage has brought the whole thing back into proper usage. It was an unlucky break, and in the true Mother Galt fashion you place the blame on yourself. In such things there is no blame: it is merely an unlucky turn of chance. You say you might have switched on the light, but since Monroe has been going up and down those steps since he was a little child he will know their every lie, especially so since he had Barry in his arms. You will go on being so proud of Monroe and this accident will in no way impair his life career; such accidents bring undesirable but strengthening pain and we ourselves become stronger having learned to brace ourselves to bear pain, we subconsciously learn to bear other things more bravely. What I'm trying to say is that don't blame yourself. In six months Monroe will be fit and well again and his experience will have developed his character and strengthened his resolve. Perhaps you think this is a callous, war induced way of looking at pain and injury. It may be but at the same time it brings comfort to the mind. I hope to write a separate letter to Monroe tonight, but give him my love and best wishes for a speedy recovery anyway. I feel that I owe him a deep gift of gratitude for pulling my share of comfort and companionship to you and papa in these passing years. When people ask me how long I have been in England now and I say "seven" I have to stop and think is it possible. Then I look at growing Lee and think it must be.

Time may march on, but she continually stretches her tentacles toward the past.

You will have had your share of nursing broken bones and soothing impatient patients. My praise and admiration goes out to you Mother --- and to both your patients of the past year. You probably feel as I did when Susan came down with the whooping-cough --- one other disease more or less to nurse actually makes little difference.

Summer is continuing to grace us with its presence. Perhaps it is England's share of your terrific heat wave now in progress. Anyway it is marvellous and I revel in it. It seems so much nicer to see the bare arms and legs of Susan and Lee. They are both becoming brown and summery in appearance.

Today was Sunday and we wanted to go to church as usual, but my hay fever was running too rampant and with continuous sneezes and swollen eyes I wasn't very presentable for church. Instead this morning Lee and Ronald dismantled one of the lean-to sections of the old stable house at the bottom of the garden as it was so old it was falling down. Ronald said it gave him some idea of just what work and danger the demolition squads are up against after a big raid. Lee of course was in his element to say nothing of Susan who was kept at a safe distance only by force. Her powers of persuasion are slowly developing, but she is still as stubborn as a mule when she wants to insist that her way of thinking is the only way. We haven't decided whether she is as stubborn as a Galt or as stubborn as a Bradbury. We share the honours equally. People ask whom she looks like as her eyes are still blue and her hair blond and she doesn't look like either Ronald or me. We assure them that she is really ours and she resembles her American grandmother in colouring. And so she does.

We have for long been trying to get Lee to go to Sunday school. He willingly accompanies us to church on his own desire made most emphatic but at the idea of Sunday school he balked. It is held in the afternoon from 2:30 to 3:30. We thought it was perhaps he thought he would miss our Sunday outing, but we assured him that we would wait until he returned. That didn't move him. In order to go he would have to go to the Abbey as our own favourite little church is three miles away and he couldn't walk there and back and we couldn't spare the petrol to take him. But he said No, that wasn't it. It came to such a crisis that this afternoon he was told he had to go. He got ready to go with Marjorie (our evacuee) and her friend. Tears rolled down his cheeks and he sobbed and he asked could he go twice to church each Sunday if we didn't make him go to Sunday School. I had to check my emotions and be harsh with him, and in the end he went with the two girls. Susan and I walked down to the Abbey to meet him as he came out. Somehow we missed him and when we got home I expected to find him still in tears. But no, he was jubilant. He liked Sunday School. He had been able to answer questions that none of the others could answer, and he had drawn a picture to illustrate today's lesson and had got a stamp to mark his attendance. He added, "It wasn't at all like what I thought it would be." When I asked him what that was, he said "Something like the hospital when I had my tonsils taken out." No wonder he had worked himself up into tears. All of which goes to show how little we know what goes on in our children's minds.

This week I have been busy making jam. I had scrounged sufficient sugar from our weekly 2½ pounds by using saccharine for sweet puddings, etc. that I could spare four pounds of what I had saved. However for this month we are getting double ration which means I can put down some gooseberry, plum, blackcurrant and raspberry jam. Also I have bottled some rhubarb without sugar. It should last through into the winter when there will be no fresh or tinned fruit. I intend to try as many available fruits as possible this way.

I'll never be able to thank you and all of those who gave toward our recent box which I gave full details in my last letter. Life has been much more worth living now I can wear silk stockings when I dress in the afternoon. Ronald kids me that this is a pretty war-attitude, but silk stockings do something to the average woman. They cast a sort of protective spell over her resolve and determination. Equally so is Lee enjoying all his "haul", and so is Marjorie.

I have spent every spare moment this week recuffing and retailing shirts for Ronald. Shirts which would normally go into the rag bag are now rehashed until they are stronger than ever - and how many coupons they save. I am getting into that frame of mind that I imagine the pioneer women have and which you two can well remember; that of creating or recreating when what we first desired wasn't at hand. It's uncanny what can be done when necessity is the mother of invention. However, I have not yet found an invention to take the place of vanishing cream, lip-stick, jello, syrup, clothes pins, candy and numerous other trifles which have disappeared or are steadily disappearing from the market. Still they are of small matter and soon forgotten.

England seems more intent than ever on the war now that Russia is in it. Our bombers are returning two-fold the hell that has been showered on England but is now relaxed for a while. We have had no sirens and there have been no big raids in this area for many a long day. We are beginning to wonder what we will do if we hear the siren again. Ronald sees much of the war work and effort in his new job and is confident that England is remounting her lost ground and that the tide has long since turned.

I have some letters to do for Ronald so I shall sign off, and hope and pray that the two of you are in good health and spirits and that your worry over Monroe has been lessened by his speedy recovery. Love to you all from all of us.

Ever your affectionate,

Opened by Examiner 5291

The family outside Holly House.

Elisabeth, Lee and Susan in the garden of Holly House.

Letter Four

Holly House
11 Quatre Bras
Hexham

Aug. 16, 1941

Mr. and Mrs. Lee Galt
125 Stanley Blvd.
Ardmore
Oklahoma, USA.

EXAMINER 6863

Dear Mother and Papa

There has been no word from you two this week, but we do hope you both continue to be well and in good spirits. The summer is drawing to its close and autumn seems just next door. The new autumnal air seems to have put extra pep (if possible) into Lee and Susan. They are both 'good' (as they call it) but so full of the joy of living that it is miraculous to behold. Today we took them to the Saturday matinee to see George Formby, the English comic star. It was Susan's second cinema jaunt as she had been to the News Theatre in Newcastle last weekend. She sat very still and absorbed as long as there was action. She timed all her reactions to those of Lee. When he laughed she roared, when he applauded, she almost fell off my lap clapping her hands.

We had given the children the chance of either seeing the big Tank Show in Newcastle or seeing George Formby. They chose the latter and I was glad, because here in Hexham they are removed from too much evidence of the war – a huge display of tanks, guns, dive bombers, etc. would only have again aroused their war curiosity.

When we went back to 'Ardmore' last weekend to collect some things, all four of us felt a little homesick for its spacious garden, modernity and freshness – but through the week there was another bad raid with five killed not so far behind us. I was glad that we hadn't succumbed to our desire to enjoy 'Ardmore' again.

There seems to be little to report as our life seems very calm and heavenly quiet at present. However, we are still undecided about our domestic help. Jenny, the housekeeper, whom I had given two weeks' trial, said she liked us personally but our house and life was too full for her. She had been keeping house for an elderly gentleman so Ronald, Lee and Susan were three lively customers for her. However, now, after the two weeks, she wants to stay, after I had already written asking Beattie to come back. Both Beattie and Jenny have their points. It's hard to choose.

Susan had a nasty accident to her middle finger on her right hand this week. The painters were painting the iron railings in front of our freshly painted house. Susan went to watch and left her hand on the front door sill. The wind blew the heavy door to and caught her hand, taking the skin off the ball of her said finger. After the first shock she has been most interested in her wound and taken most meticulous care of it.

I must get busy with Susan's winter outfits. Luckily, I had material laid aside before clothes rationing, so her winter coat and leggings will be coupon free. As for her many dresses needed, I shall re-make some of the dresses in your last box. It seems a shame to tear up such perfect young ladies' dresses to make clothes for a little girl but one has to do drastic things these days.

We are hoping that Mother and Father Bradbury will come to visit us in September – the first time since war began. Travel is very difficult these days and we are urged not to travel – but we do want them to visit us.
Ronald is busier than ever these days and from reports of his reports to London, his work is both effective and appreciated.

The Hospital work progresses as the wards seem to expand each week. There were three mastoids in this week. How my heart went out to them!

In one of your next letters would you send a few bobby pins (Kirby grips - or hair grips) as we are unable to get any and Susan and I are both almost without. Otherwise we have everything we need. In fact we're sitting pretty. Very pretty.

    All our love and kisses -
    Elisabeth

Beattie's story – letter from Beattie herself to Sue Newton in 2010.

Dear Sue,

How nice to receive your letter, I don't mind you using my life with the Bradbury family as long as you send me a copy of the book.

How to start. I don't know how long this letter will be or how long it will take me to write it.

When I finished school in 1938 I went to work for Mrs Bootiman, she was very old and lived with her crippled son and was a Dr's widow, after a while she told me she had been talking to a Mrs Bradbury who was expecting a baby and already had a son and she was looking for someone to help with the children and she thought it should be me and so I entered Ardmore and met the Bradbury family.

After you were born, the war began and your Dad wanted his family safe. But also working in the household was Christie Pemberton who did the cooking and housework, but only one of us could go with your parents, when it was made known it was me she didn't speak to me anymore; however our first stop was at Otterburn Hall where your Dad rented a gardener's cottage but we didn't stay there long. About 10 yrs ago I visited Otterburn Hall but it was nothing like I remembered it.

Next we went to Hexham where we had a few rooms off the Rector called Mr Farghar, he was old and crotchety and complained about the noise we made so we moved to Holly house. There was a building at the bottom of the garden where we kept hens and another building attached to the house where we kept rabbits, this supplemented our meat ration and the eggs where put in a bucket of isinglass so we always had eggs during the autumn months. We went looking for orchards and getting fruit which we botted also your mum got an allotment where we grew vegetables, at that time she had a little black car and we would call at the cooperative stables and pick up a bag of manure, so you can imagine what the car smelt like. Also to furnish Holly House your Dad went to the auction rooms in Hexham.

I learnt a lot from your mum, she was like a second mother to me. I learnt how to love gardening, sewing and cooking.

At that time, there was lots of soldiers stationed in Hexham, mostly Border Regiment & Anzacs and every Christmas they invited a soldier to dinner. I remember one called Tommy Tittal who drank wine with his dinner and said 'Eek I'm floatin'.

Then we went to London, 'Golders Green' it was there I got my calling up papers, and I had to report to the Labours Exchange. When I went there she asked me what I wanted to do. When I said I wanted to go nursing she told me there was no vacancy's all she had was for a cleaner to clean the hostels the munition workers used. Personally I think when she heard my north country accent she thought I would fall for her suggestion but I said no, I'd go home and see what I could find and so I started my nursing career.

I do hope what your mother wrote to your grandmother about me was good. I know your mother liked my accent and some of the north country sayings I said,

Hope to hear from you soon, love
Beattie

Sketch of Lee and Beattie in 1943, drawn by Beattie's father.

Letter Five

                                              Holly House
                                                    Hexam
                                                  Sept, 6, 1941

    If I don't receive a letter from some of the Ardmore family soon, I will reverse your mental tactics and think that it is you who have been bombed out of existence. It is now over four weeks since word came through from you. Either the carrying ships have gone down, or they shall all arrive at once. Regardless, I do hope that all goes well with both of you.

    However apologies are also on my side as last week did not give me time to get the usual weekly bulleting out to you, so here goes for a nice long one that may keep you going for the time being. My accumulated family is all properly placed and quiet --- the first time today --- so I can concentrate on writing. Lee is bedded down on an army coat in our room, thrilled because it is the kind of bed that soldiers sleep on, if they do sleep on beds. Susan is tucked in her cot in the nursery, where the blackout is not put up yet, as she begs so hard to leave the shutters off. It means an extra trip up to the nursery later when blackout time is reached, which grows sooner every evening. Ronald is reading. Father Bradbury is reading and Mother Bradbury is knitting. The latter came on Wednesday and hoped to be with us almost a week. It is almost two years since Mother Bradbury has seen Susan, for she saw Lee when Ronald took him to Whaley Bridge last fall. It is good to have them with us, to share the children, and to see Holly House for themselves. I am hoping that they will write you a letter when they leave so that you two can, in some way, share their visit and pretend it was yours as well. The two war years have made them look older, and Mother is walking very badly as she has trouble with her feet. However, she is enjoying Hexham and the children and Father is getting in some good fishing on the admirable stretches of the Tyne.

    We left Lee playing in the garden, and Susan asleep for her daytime nap, and Beattie getting the dinner while we four went to our little church up the valley. Today was a special day of prayer as it is the third September of the war. If our concentrated prayers are answered the war should be well on its way to completion. This afternoon Lee went to Sunday School at the Abbey while Susan and I waited for him in the adjoining park. The rest of the crew was sleeping off the Sunday dinner. Lee does enjoy his Sunday School. His eyes sparkle and his voice seems deeper and even more meaningful as he tries to tell us all the things they did at the service.

Beside the typewriter is a large bowl of lovely, ripe Victorian plums, about the first fruit which I have been able to indulge in a long time. Always before, if there has been any chance, stray fruit that drifted to Hexham, I saved it for the children. But now the two plum trees, which are heavily laden in the back garden, are yielding their produce, and the plums are too good to be true. I have made some plum jam and I hope to bottle quite a lot as well. Lee and Susan have eaten so many they should be sick but they are not.

Aerial activity in the Northeast has suddenly leapt to life, and it has given much excitement and much to talk about. Two weeks ago tomorrow when I went through to Cleadon to pick up Beattie, who was returning to our fold, I took Lee and Susan with me. There was a raid with machine gunning and bombs, and it was remarkable how no one paid any attention to that was happening above and merely carried on.

The next section has been tampered with by the authorities.
".... Has its first real blitz, with ... We heard nothing of it here but Ronald gave first hand information of it when he went into town the next day. He was posted for extra watch the next night as they expected a .... , but nothing further has happened."

I had been in on the Friday before to see if my eyes needed glasses, as I had had several bad headaches and Ronald thought I might need glasses for sewing and reading. The specialist, however, said I had about the best eyesight he had ever tested, and attributed the headaches to the severe hay fever I had had this summer. The home and surgery of this specialist did not exist the ... (tampered with) afterwards as a huge bomb dropped just by. It is dreadful to think of how many and unnecessary non-military objects are hit. When I did my rounds on the following Wednesday at the hospital, many fresh beds appeared filled with some of the raid victims who, though battered and torn, were just as brave and determined as ever.

The next news of our family is that Ronald has been given a big promotion in the Ministry of Labour in the Northeast and is now one of the Big Shots, having much responsibility and doing even more vital work in the supply of labour and completion of government projects than before. He was promoted over older and more experienced men in that field, so he must have something that the government considers vital and precious to them. He is extremely pleased and excited about his promotion, as he has reason to be.

Lee's school starts again tomorrow and he is anxious to get back to the grindstone, although he has more than enjoyed his holiday. It seems to have given a breathing space in which to leap up three inches, gain breadth and a more manly appearance. Susan is still keeping him up to scratch with a good race. What happy times they have together. We tease Susan because she can't say her R's properly. Tonight in the bath Lee was trying to make her say, "Round the ragged rocks", but all that came out was "lound the lagged locks" which produced great roars from lee as well as from me.

Two parcels arrived from Irene Mints from Chicago, containing six tins of dehydrated fruit and vegetables, which were both new and most welcome to us. They shall go in our iron-ration cupboard to be used in an emergency. I found out last week that any parcels weighing over seven pounds are not sent to the person to whom they are addressed, but to the Red Cross. There may be some rhyme and reason for this but it seems hard after all the care, trouble and expense the sender has gone to, to have his personal gift turned into public property. But we can't really complain because this war belongs to all of us, and we must share alike of both luxuries and miseries. I think it is this knowledge that all do share alike and that none of us are privileged that makes everything so much easier to bear.

Our hens are still doing remarkably well and the allotment is putting forth some admirable attempts. This week the French beans have just come into their own, and we have revelled in them as much as we have in the abundant plums. I have put pounds of these beans, already sliced and prepared, away in salt for winter use. There should be sufficient vegetables in the garden to stand the winter and we won't be so thin in that line as we were last winter when we had no allotment from which to draw.

Our evacuee returns to us tomorrow after her holidays spent at the coast. She has come through safely, but she has gone through much that she need not have experienced and I am glad that she can return to us where her schooling can go on uninterrupted. Susan and Lee are looking forward to her return.

This just about covers the news, so I shall sign off for this time, hoping both of you are extremely well and fit. Rest assured that all of us are - we are still too 'fighting mad' to be anything else but fit. The children send love and kisses. It would warm your hearts to know how proud Ronald is of his American wife, and Lee of his American Mother these days. Not that they have not always been proud, but it has just been brought home to them just what greatness there is in the heart of America.

All our love and kisses.

Affectionately, Elisabeth

Letter Six

Holly House

Mar 22, 1942

To Mr. and Mrs. Lee Galt
125 Stanley Blvd.
Ardmore, Oklahoma, USA

No Examiner number

Dear Mother and Papa

A No letter week, as there is no news to comment upon. I trust you both are well and that legs and colds are well under control. This lovely spring weather, which I am sure you are enjoying has probably given you a new life as it has us. It's so grand to work out of doors again, to feel the sun, turn the soil, discover the first shoots and buds. Ronald, Beattie and I have worked the flower garden into shape here at Holly House and have half-done the allotment digging. Lee and Susan have worked with us. Yesterday at the allotment Susan was collecting potatoes that Ronald came across as he dug – over-looked ones. Lee was collecting artichokes that Beattie forked up - and Dinah was well at my heels as I thinned and forked raspberry canes. It was all hands out!

Today has been great excitement for the children and Marjorie as Hexham had a mock invasion today. As we are one main artery and an important barricade is near us, they all saw plenty of activity and heard even more with guns, fake bombs and tanks. The Home Guard seem to have worked out a real picture of what might still someday happen.

Speaking of shooting, we have brought our air-gun through from 'Ardmore' and Ronald has put up a target and range for Lee in the back garden. Even Susan insists upon her try and it's quite a contest. Susan has also mastered her trike in grand style and all of us go for rides – quite a brigade with five or six cycles scampering along. It's very good of Susan to work the bike at all because the pedals are off (it is Lee's old one and has seen hard wear) and the single bar is tricky to stick onto. Lee has taught her all the tricks of the trade and she can turn sharp corners in two and go everywhere. I don't know who is prouder of Susan - Lee or Susan, herself!

This week we had the chimney sweep in which meant spring cleaning all over again. Coal fires are fine but their aftermath is a very dirty affair. I'm saving the soot for the garden.

We are renting 'Ardmore' unfurnished which means we have to bring that house load of furniture through to Holly House. We are choosing the best of the two lots which should make Holly House superb – then we'll send the rest to the Auction Room.

Ronald has been so busy this week he has hardly had time to breathe. Two of his second-class officers have been ill, so he's been doing three men's work. He says he never has time to stop all day long – what a job!

He killed one of our oldest hens to cut down our numbers and how beautifully it roasted. It was delicious tasting chicken after so long.

The other hens are beginning their good spring lay after their winter rest and it's good to have enough eggs once again. I hope to put down even more than I did last year.
Lee and Susan are both well. We are still looking forward to the latter's tonsils coming out. The Dr. is arranging it soon. Those imps are up to all tricks and sayings these days. Lee is going ahead at school by leaps and bounds. He's always telling us about 'our form', 'our school', etc. - so much so that Susan now has an imaginary school. The stories she tells are equal to Lee's. Tonight when Susan was put to bed she came out with 'Open Sesame'. She meant for me to open my arms and give her a big hug. Tonight in the bathroom, while I was bathing them, Ronald asked if "Nekko" was rationed (it's a medicated soap) and Susan said "No, Daddy an echo is in a valley not in a shop." She has answers to everything.

Everyone seems brighter now that MacArthur has gone to Australia. In the American commentary to this country last night all the anti-British criticism in America was discussed freely. I think this should be so for there's an answer to everyone if anyone will look for it. Still, doubts and criticism are good because they bring out the truths.

To explain Pearl Harbour, Singapore and Java defeats brings us to the fact that we've a hard pull ahead of us but combined we'll pull through. Statistics surely can't fail us – our production in 1943 will give us the materials we want, to win.

Beattie has to register next Saturday. She is 17 and would like to be in one of the Forces but is too young, according to her Mother. We'll have to wait to see if she is called.

It's now time so I'll sign off. Keep care of yourselves and write us often.

Love from Lee and Susan – and all of us.

Affectionately yours
Elisabeth

Lee Bradbury

Letter Seven

Holly House

Dec. 27, 1942

To Mr. and Mrs. Lee Galt
125 Stanley Blvd.
Ardmore, Oklahoma, USA

Dear Mother and Papa

It is the Sunday after Christmas and there is a suggestion of calming down in the atmosphere of Holly House. What tremendous excitement, activity and sheer joy the children have claimed this time. I think it was because there was so little outside one's home to afford a Christmas atmosphere – that we had to have so much inside. For weeks we had been making and assembling toys for them. As Lee said afterwards - "So many of the gang got just money. I'm glad Santa Claus managed to give us something more than just money – 'cause there isn't anything to buy anyway."

Their show around the Christmas tree was indeed a show. Susan had a completely furnished four room doll's house, a kitchen cabinet, dishes, a doll, school-girl's shoulder purse and additional ends. Lee's main object was a very superior punch ball and two pairs of boxing gloves. (His action is quite good and he knows how to handle a punch ball.) Not forgetting of course – their most important present. Topsy, a puppy. Dinah, as you know, is getting quite old and is interested only in me and in sleep. The fun in her seems to have settled down – so a puppy was called for. Topsy is a Manchester Terrier – supposedly – but with a little mixture of Liverpool and Stockport put in, as Ronald says. He's the colour of milk and bitter chocolate – well marked - and very pert. What fun the children do have with it. Beattie and I are battling nobly with the housebreaking problem and hope to win a victory soon.

A turkey was given to us – and we considered ourselves very lucky as they were indeed scarce. I had made a grand cake (not the old Christmas recipe – but one with carrot, apple, soya flour and only one pound of fruit – I used the raisins Mildred had sent to Susan – and it was really a good disguise). The plum pudding was a made-up one as well –

but it tasted just as usual and no one knew the difference.

Mrs. Bull (her Ph.D husband now serving in the South) and her daughter, and two soldiers stationed locally made up our noon-day meal – then two more children (Sally Page – Tom's daughter – and Ian Sinclair) joined us, together with Dr. Crowthers, the children's much beloved dentist - all joined us for tea. Oh, but there was a grand party of games beforehand with all the grownups being as much a child as any of the younger lot! The tea was a great success with mince pies, sausage rolls, assorted sandwiches, cup cakes, cheese straws, Christmas cake – and a double layer whipped jelly! How the children's eyes popped at the latter (again, Mildred's present to Susan).

Susan said to thank you for her Xmas dress as it was made out of the two odd skirts you had sent in the two parcels. The dress was out of the white corduroy with a Peter Pan blouse made out of the yellow skirt. With white socks and a yellow hair ribbon, she did look sweet – and Lee called her a glamour girl.

The children were put to bed at seven but the rest of the party carried on with odd grownup games. It was a jolly time - made possible by the joy of the war news – the feeling of success, advance and fruitful hopes – rather than just longing!

The New Year seems to promise great things and we are working just as hard as ever to attain them. Austerity is good for the soul!

Ronald is feeling much better and I am so grateful for it was a pity to see him in such pain. Kidney trouble can be so bothersome. At present he's looking better than he has for a long time. The loss of weight (war-time diet and walking – no car) is an asset as you can imagine! As for me – I'm fine and never am ill. Lee and I are those people who seem immune and we gallop through the winters. Susan is much better this winter with her tonsils out. If she does get a snuffly cold it vanishes as quickly as it came without earache, etc. It is a relief!

Ronald gave me two lovely mantel clocks for Xmas. You can't buy clocks for love or money in shops as they don't exist - and you can't get broken ones mended because there are no spare parts with which to mend them. He had a brainwave and inserted an advertisement and found two lovely, eight day clocks – just like new – and what a blessing to have a clock to tell time by and not have to rely on the sun (of which there is none) and the wireless programs.

It's bed time and I'll say a fond goodnight. Do keep well and bright for us, for the cheeriness of your constant letters mean much to us all. May the New Year be kind, generous and good to you.

Love and kisses
Your own , Elisabeth

Letter Eight

Holly House
Mar 4 1943

To Mr. and Mrs. Lee Galt
125 Stanley Blvd.
Ardmore, Oklahoma, USA

Dear Mother and Papa

If the writing should be crooked and the sentences disjointed, blame it on your grand-daughter Susan, as I am writing this perched on the edge of the armchair before the nursery fire. Susan gets very bored with herself at this time of day (just before tea) and finds her isolation a bit trying. She also has a pad and a pencil and is writing you a line – very in earnest but not very good.

We thought it most unlikely that Susan would escape chicken-pox seeing that Lee had it so badly, but she didn't escape – she passed with flying colours. Lee had a bad dose and was quite ill and lifeless for about a week but got better only to have the glands behind his ears swell because he had so many spots in his hair. Then Susan came down with them – hundreds more than Lee so it seemed. She couldn't shut her eyes they were peppered so with them. But after four or five days when the fever and the accompanying irritation was gone, she felt much better – but still in bed. Then the next morning I thought her face looked very flushed all over with a pin-prick rash covering her body. I thought it was Scarlet Fever and called the Dr. Unfortunately he had a delivery on his hands and I had to wait several hours. How relieved I was to find it was only some kind of supplementary skin rash caused by so much boracic dusting etc. of her spots. I had visualized them taking her to the Fever Hospital for a month – then the same thing again with Lee. My relief knew no bounds, and I was almost weak with joy. Today – two days afterwards her blush is gone, the rash has died and she is as right as rain except for the pox scabs which keep coming off to her consternation. She thinks she's losing something!

As Lee has been fumigated and not in contact with Susan he started school today, having been away a day over 3 weeks. He says it seems a long time. This morning after breakfast I re-read him your two letters which came yesterday. He said, "I wish I could be near Papa in America then he wouldn't feel so poorly and old as he says he does. I'd cheer him up." Then he wanted to know if burst pipes in America were just the same as those in England. He said he could help Gran-Gran do that too. He's a regular handyman in his own estimation. But he and Ronald are always making or fixing something.

Ronald has been doing a perspective (draughted the colour with water colour) of a war-time housing scheme the firm has done for a northern factory. It was the first time Lee had ever seen Ronald at work on a drawing board and he has been fascinated that so marvellous a result could come forward with just Daddy working on paper.

The day before Susan took ill and Lee was up but not near other children – Beattie and I took them, Lee on his run bike and Susan on the chair in front of mine – to a nearby dene where we gathered moss, fern and plants for a moss garden to decorate our dining table. It was lovely in the woods and the children did enjoy it. Lee couldn't pass by so much would-be fire wood without gathering some, so we came away with Susan holding a huge bundle in her lap, and equal bundles strapped in over 3 bikes. Lee assured me we had saved no end of fuel for the war effort and so we did.

Spring has definitely come because I saw the first blossom out today. The weather has been so mild and so short it seems almost a miracle. Most of us haven't started our allotments yet although I hope to set mine this week and trust that a late frost doesn't come. North of England weather is a guessing riddle!

Papa, it was pathetic to read you were feeling so down-hearted. You mustn't! You have had your share of activity and must now just take it easy. It's nature's compensation for so arduous a life. It would really be terrible if we really had to work hard when we grow old. So relive the days when you were so active and get your present pleasure from them. There's a lot of wisdom, life and enjoyment left in our armchair life!

Mother, I'm glad you keep on finding burst pipes, shrubs, etc. to occupy you. There is a certain satisfaction found nowhere else, in just keeping one's home in order.

And you mustn't worry about us as there is nothing to worry about. We're fine, healthy and strong – the war is winning its way to a well-earned end – and someday we'll all pay our visit to you. What goes on between now and then – we'll just make that time the more precious. So keep smiling as you have done these past six years since Lee and I saw you. We love you more dearly than ever.

Ronald said to say hello and give you his love if I wrote this before he came home from the office. He's feeling better now spring has come and his working hours don't seem so long now black-out is shorter.

All our love and best wishes! Kisses from Lee and Susan
Your, Elisabeth

Letter Nine

Holly House
May 30 1943

To Mr. and Mrs. Lee Galt
125 Stanley Blvd.
Ardmore, Oklahoma, USA

Dear Mother and Papa

This week brought a cheery letter from you, full of chickens. Your venture sounds great – a good war effort and a source of pleasure to you as well. Hope you have all the success you deserve with it.

I'm taking time off from my house guests to write this. We have had so many visitors since Ronald left, as friends have taken pity on us and are keeping us company. Kathie Page came out last week-end, then from Monday to Friday Beattie's sister-in-law and niece, and this weekend Nan, Stan and Ellie Blackwood, our old neighbours at Cleadon. How glad I was Kathie was out last weekend as she missed a severe raid at her home with much loss of porperty and lives. Yet – everyone is smiling. "Just so much Hitler" they say and carry on.

Poor Nan has been very ill with the nerves in her face reacting wrong and it's pitiful to see her in such pain when eating and talking. I will hate to leave all our Northern friends but London isn't so far away.

I'm going down to London tomorrow to help look and decide upon a house. Ronald has about ten in view – all reasonably safe, secure, and much what we want. A friend is coming in to be with Beattie and the children while I'm away. They'll manage fine without me.
I asked Mother and Father Bradbury if they would like Lee and Susan while we moved but they haven't been too well and had to decline the offer. They say it's just old age and the present food – but I do feel they are seriously 'getting down'. I wish I could do something to cheer them up. I must congratulate you two; through all your mishaps you still keep your spirits up and your chins high. However, I feel it that I can't be near you when you need me or I could be of use to you. I pray my letters give some help, but I'm sure it's very little.

I'm enclosing a drawing Ronald enclosed in a letter for the children; they did laugh at it! They both are in splendid health – glowing with it, in fact. They've had a gay time with so many people staying with us. They are both so loving and friendly!

The weather has been perfect this week as well! We are all quite brown and always warm. It is a great joy!

It's getting time to put the guests to bed for the night, so I'll say a fond goodnight and hope and pray you both are well.

Kisses from Lee and Susan
All my love
Ever your,
Elisabeth

Letter Ten

8 Thornton Way
LONDON
N.W.11

August 30, 1943

To Mr. and Mrs. Lee Galt
125 Stanley Blvd.
Ardmore, Oklahoma, USA

Dear Mother and Papa

We await further letters from you, but know they will all come together when a convoy comes through. I do hope you both are well and full of the joy of living. It has been a lovely summer in London, the nicest I've ever known in England. It's so grand to feel summer as well as to see it on the calendar. However, the second extra hour is now removed and black-out comes far too soon for the lovely evenings.

Lee and Susan thrive on the life here – are ever so well, and so full of vim and vigour. Their new friends, new surroundings and the novelty of London are all to their liking. Last Saturday we went into town to meet Ronald, and he took us to Madame Toussaud's, the famous wax works museum. I don't know when I've laughed so hard! It was at Susan, whom Ronald told to go up to one of the attendants and ask the way. Of course, it was a wax figure but so life-like she didn't realise it. She got up her courage and asked the question but when no answer came she was taken aback. When we explained she gave the figure the most curious look. A little further on there was a live attendant identical in detail, who posed as if he were a dumb statue. Susan wasn't going to be fooled this time and was just on the verge of punching him to see if he were real, when he checked her under the chin. She fairly jumped out of her skin and the rest of us rocked with laughter. Lee did enjoy the historical tableau and he knew far more about the historical details and events than I did. These were too deep for Susan, but she did like the Sleeping Beauty that was rigged out with a bosom that heaved with every artificial breath she took. Quite a scene.

Earlier in the week, the children, Beattie and I armed with four carriers containing all seven lively pups went again into town to sell the litter. They were so sweet and lovely it was a shame to part with them but war-time feeding of dogs is difficult. The pet shop which had half promised to buy them was full with pedigree dogs and wouldn't look at my mongrels, so we had to ask sufficient policemen until we did locate a buyer. As I did years ago with Francis, spend the money from her babes on a safeguard operation, I shall do the same with Topsy. Topsy is so exuberant and dashing these days now the burden of the pups is removed, that it's like having a new playmate for the children. She has the world's sweetest disposition.

Sunday we went by bus – a long interesting ride – to the famous Epping Forest. On the rolling fields edging the forest there was a meeting of a 'model airplane' club. Lee was as interested as any actual member, and when one large model soared and vanished far into the forest – it was a triumph for him. We walked through the forest and discovered there were lots of blackberries to be picked. Susan ate till she popped – but the rest of us were dutiful and picked for bottling and jam.

Last week saw Susan and Lee both having their interviews with their headmistress and headmaster and being shown over their schools. Susan met Miss Ironside on Tuesday, was given a simple oral test and as she wasn't a bit shy put herself over well. It was decided she is beyond kindergarten and will go into the beginners' class. Lee was very manly and subdued at his interview but it went off well. He liked the building and the house-captain scheme. I know they both will be happy – but changing schools and teachers is always a bit frightening. Susan will take special dancing which she is looking forward to with great interest.

Luckily a neighbour is moving and I have been allocated his allotment. The allotments originally were grass tennis courts, planned in among the rose beds – so now as you dig you couldn't imagine more heavenly surroundings. Today I put in broccoli, cauliflower, sprouts and cabbage. My leeks, spinach, radishes, parsley and lettuce which were planted some time ago are amazing. The soil is good-growing and the weather far more helpful than in the North. We have also gained permission to have chickens (in pre-war days bye-laws of the Suburb did not permit the keeping of poultry) so if we can resurrect some wire and unearth some pullets we should have our own eggs again. The eggs put down in water glass came through the move without a single breakage. How we are enjoying them.

We had hoped Mother and Father Bradbury would come to visit us before school started but they don't feel well enough to travel. They seem so 'down' these days these days, I only wish I could do something to cheer them up. What about you two? I always feel you are bright and happy, and hope it isn't just wishful thinking.

One day last week I took the children to visit Cousin Joyce (Ronald's 1st cousin) who has two children as well. It's nice living near Ronald's relatives, for we have been so long so far away from any relatives who could visit us or whom we could visit. We feel claimed again.

Tomorrow I'm taking Lee into town to Peter Robinson's (big store) for his new school uniform. If we're through in time I shall take him to his first real theatre. It's great having a son old enough to escort me!

War news grows better and fiercer each day. We are still awaiting vital results of the Quebec conference. It's interesting watching the flow of planes on the bomber route to Italy. Their mess and might are being felt.

Do keep care of yourselves.

We send you all our love and special kisses from Lee and Susan
Ever your,
Elisabeth

8 Thornton Way, London.

Letter Eleven

8 Thornton Way
LONDON
N.W.11

September 14, 1943

To Mr. and Mrs. Lee Galt
125 Stanley Blvd.
Ardmore, Oklahoma, USA

Dear Mother and Papa

A very quick letter of yours came through today, breaking all records for coming over in thirteen days. That's short of a miracle in war time. Sorry to hear the heat had depleted your energy. I knew it must be hot at home for London to have been so delightfully warm. We are still having week-end afternoon teas in the garden and it's heavenly.

The past week has been a full one as Ronald has been on his annual week's leave. We have been so upset by his family's pathetic and down-hearted letters that he went first to spend half his week with them. It was impossible for the rest of us to go as Mother B would have been neither well enough or able (rations, etc.) to cope with us. However, Ronald found them better than he had expected and his visit cheered them up sufficiently that they have promised to come see us and are due to arrive tomorrow. Mother B said she had written you a long letter in January but as you have never mentioned even receiving it, I'm sure it must have gone down. Perhaps she'll write you another while they're here and we'll also take some snaps to show you all of us and 8 Thornton Way.

The rest of Ronald's week was spent here with the family
'doing' London some more. They do enjoy these trips, to say nothing of our enjoying their reactions. Did I tell you I had taken Lee to see a play? I've promised Susan some Russian ballet as she is starting dancing this term and wants to know all about it.

Susan's school starts tomorrow and she is all ready with her pencil box packed, her tunic and blouse pressed, her blazer cleaned, her shoe bag (with Susan Bradbury written and embroidered on it) packed with gym shoes and ballet slippers. Her mental make-up is just as ready as she is raring to go. Lee's school starts two days later and he too is all ready! More power to them and bless their quivering hearts for big new schools are an exciting experience.

Over the week-end we had Don and Isabel Reid staying with us, and we were joined for Saturday tea and supper by Ralph Pickwick - all of us knew each other in N.Y. - all being English men who married American wives. Unfortunately Ralph's wife, Barbara, was home with their young daughter at the outbreak of the war and she has been unable to get back over. I'm sure it hurt him to see our complete and happy household, while he suffered through his being divided! Don and Isabel were as grand as ever and we did so enjoy their visit. Douglas Hill, the other member of the N.Y. Gang is at present in the U.S., having gone over in a bomber. He is now 2nd in command of England's cotton industry. Odd that all the men of that crowd should be in government work. Minds recognised, I presume!

Beattie has had her interview with the Ministry of Labour official today and she is to be leaving within the next two weeks. She is disappointed as she wanted to go into nursing but since she is trained as a domestic servant they are directing and training her as a cook either to a hospital or hostel! I think she's more disappointed that she won't be in uniform.

While Ronald was away I spent some hours in the garden doing the final digging to the flowerbeds. Recent rains had softened the clay soil so that with perseverance I was successful. The garden is well stocked with roses and they are having a long and delightful season. I like too the golden privet hedge that borders the terrace leading onto the French doors at the back. The lawn which was a hay field when we came is now a lovely smooth green through persistent cutting and rolling. We've had out the croquet set again and the running is very fast!

Ronald and I have had batteries fitted onto our bikes so we can do night cycling. It's an odd, and wholly delightful, sensation cycling at night. I often wonder how we'll go back to the passive acceptance of cars after the exuberant thrill of cycling as a means of travelling.

I'm glad you have all your rooms and apartments rented as it should have word) kept you occupied with something to do and the means by which to do it. But don't rent the roof off your head, as you both deserve to be ever so comfortable in these present years. Are your financial worries any less or do you still have to figure out taxes, etc.! I was always sure I would be able to help you in later years but Allied efforts seem to come before personal ones and I suppose that's right. I think you understand!

The war news continues superb although Mussolini has done the disappearing trick and Italy is dizzy with her capitulations. You can feel still greater things in the air.

The children send their love and kisses and Ronald joins me in offering our undying devotion. Take care of yourselves for our sakes.

Ever your affectionate,
Elisabeth

Lee and Susan starting their new schools in London.

Letter Twelve

8 Thornton Way
LONDON
N.W.11

September 26, 1943

To Mr. and Mrs. Lee Galt
125 Stanley Blvd.
Ardmore, Oklahoma, USA

Dear Mother and Papa

No letter from you this week to answer so this will be a one-sided newsletter. However I do hope you both continue to be fit, well and happy! Our news of the week was the end of Mother and Father Bradbury's visit and the departure of Beattie! Mother and Father B. had a full week with us and they were as thrilled with our new home as we are. Of course, Mother B still claims London as her home for although she has not really lived here for 43 years she's a Londoner at heart! The children enjoyed their visit. What with the excitement of their being here and that of starting school Lee and Susan were keyed up. However they have settled down again and take schools for granted and not as novelties now. Lee's Prep School believes in work for at the age of 8¼ he has begun Latin, Algebra and Geometry. It seems only yesterday he learned to read. I wish you could see him, Papa – he sits hours over the Children's Encyclopaedia

as you do over the dictionary. He also started the Cubs, our Junior Boy Scouts. This thrill carried him over the disappointment of finding he had to attend school on Saturday morning. He doesn't come home each day until 20 minutes to five as they do their homework at school. It's quite a system and a thorough school.

Susan is still walking on air because of her 'proper' school. I told you they had put her in the beginners and not kindergarten. She's elated! Her first dancing lesson is this week. She thinks she'll be able to do ballet after one lesson! A parcel of outgrown clothes arrived for Susan from Dorothy Gifford Hart and Susan was overjoyed. They fit beautifully and she did so need them.

Yes, Beattie departed this week, having reached 19 years, and being a mobile woman worker now. The Employment Exchange said she would probably be posted as a cook to a hospital canteen after an 8 weeks course. I am tending the house, shopping, etc. Quite easy to manage as I've cut it down to a fine system. Auntie Vin has promised to come over and spend an occasional night with us to allow us to get out sometime.

We took the children into town to see the R.A.F. Exhibition and they did enjoy it – Lee especially liked the supposed flight over Germany and the exploring of the loading barge. Susan liked the horror photographs which turned Lee and me! I think she must be going to be a Doctor or a nurse!

Ronald is still very fit. His constant loss of weight is much to his advantage and he's looking and feeling much better than he has for years. He does like working in London! His work is steady and engrossing. I, too – feel very fit. In fact London seems to like us as we like her.

We all send you love and kisses and hope you both are top rate!

All our love –
Your –
Elisabeth

Letter Thirteen

8 Thornton Way
LONDON
N.W.11

October 13 1943

To Mr. and Mrs. Lee Galt
125 Stanley Blvd.
Ardmore, Oklahoma, USA

Dear Mother and Papa

I am certain it is literally 'ages' since last we heard from you. I do hope and pray you both are in fine fettle and good spirits. We talk of you, think of you and are with you so in spirit that I know you must feel us there.

All of us are in miraculous spirit and health. London seems to have rejuvenated Ronald and me and to have put even more vim and vigour (if possible) into Lee and Susan. They are both so well settled in their schools. I must take a snap of Susan to show you the typical English school girl in tunic of blue. I wonder if I was as thrilled as a small girl with school as she is. She wants to go so early that one morning she found the door still locked. I don't think she realized it had doors!

Lee's school is a mixture of very modern ideas and the conventional ones as well. They seem to pile on the work but he likes it and delights in all the things he's learning. It's grand to see him taking over my place of reading stories and comics to Susan. He does enjoy his soccer which they play instead of rugger. I can't imagine either of them any happier than they are at present. The same goes for all of us. I feel far more worthwhile now that Beattie is gone and I no longer merely pilot but run the whole ship as well. True, I have no time for hospital work or such, but my war job is being self sufficient within our own household. I have my allotment already feeding me and am getting it into winter garb prior to the needed frosts.

Ronald's work and project moves steadily on and although the work is slow and tedious when once the time is ripe for its full development it will move with a swing.

For the next few days he's paying a visit to Scotland on a special investigation. I only hope he won't find the travelling too tedious.

Last weekend we had Mr. Edwards, Lee's god-father, who has just been created Professor Edwards, to spend a few days with us on his way to Cambridge. We were anxious to show him our new home and surroundings and he was overjoyed. Everyone is always so pleasantly surprised because it's all so much nicer than even words can describe. While he was here we spent a long afternoon at Kew Gardens, a marvel to behold! Last weekend we took the children to see the famous Mart held every Sunday at Petticoat Lane and distict. Seeing is hardly believing and their eyes saw so much of life they fairly burst. It is indeed an education in itself, just living in London. I think the thing they like best is the great quantity of escalators or moving stairs. This modern invention is in its numerous and frequent uses (some terribly long in the tube stations) offers them more amusement than anything else. Then too they like the Heath at our doorstep with its woods, fields, playgrounds and numerous advantages.

I have just finished Mr. Willkie's One World and did so enjoy it, feeling not only that I knew a bit of his one world but a bit of the man who focused it into view.

Do keep your spirits high. We love you and are ever so near, though far the distance. Keep well.

All our love and kisses.
Your,
Elisabeth

Letter Fourteen

8 Thornton Way
LONDON
N.W.11

October 14, 1943

To Mr. and Mrs. Lee Galt
125 Stanley Blvd.
Ardmore, Oklahoma, USA

Dear Mother and Papa

Your letter received this morning telling of Papa's month's illness. I do hope he is better now and that you two are again enjoying your calm days together. I know good health can't be forever – but I always hope for it. Both of you are so close in my thoughts and prayers. Take care of yourself as well.

I posted you a long letter yesterday so this will be just a note. Two of your letters came yesterday and today. One was written on Aug. 5 and the other on Sept. 5 so it goes to show how they accumulate for a convoy.

Sorry about Cecil and his shop but it's one of those war necessities. His knowledge and experience would be greatly needed and appreciated at an air-war base. How many have had to change horses in mid-stream – but all to the best in the end.

Auntie Viv spent last night with us and she has promised to write you a letter about your grandchildren.

It's time for me to go join the queues for today's shopping so I'll say a fond cheerio and I do hope Papa is better and you yourself are rested.

All my love and more,
Your
Elisabeth

Letter Fifteen

8 Thornton Way
LONDON
N.W.11

December 13, 1943

To Mr. and Mrs. Lee Galt
125 Stanley Blvd.
Ardmore, Oklahoma, USA

Dear Mother and Papa

It seems several weeks since last we heard from you. I do hope you both are well and having a mild winter with no illness. I do not know whether you have had the 'flu epidemic as we have had. It's been rather a game of here today and in bed tomorrow. I thought our family was going to be lucky and miss it, but Susan blotted our copy book when she fell ill last Friday. Her temperature raged and soared (104°) but at the end of 48 hours it had left her and she was her same happy self again. It's done her no harm except postponing her birthday party which was a blow as I had saved (sugar, fats, fruit) in order to bake for the party and had done said baking when Susan came home from school. So there was no party, but much party food. Some of the stuff will keep so it isn't too bad! Our other item of special interest to you is that I got in touch with Col. Clarence Breedlove – Ruth's brother – through the American post office and he came to see us last Sunday. As the first visitor from Ardmore since our sojourn over here almost 10 years ago – it was quite an occasion. He seemed to enjoy his visit and indeed we enjoyed him. He was splendid with the children, filling Lee with all the air force stories he would like to hear – and teasing Susan. He has two children just their ages back in Oklahoma.
Last week we had another visitor – John Walkden from Edinburgh – Lee's second god-father. It was the Walkdens we once spent a summer with in Wales. Being in London and the centre of things, brings many friends to see us, whom we haven't seen for years.

Lee and Susan's schools break up this week for Christmas holidays and it has been a successful term for both of them. Lee's printed exam paper fairly astounded us in what he was expected to know. He's Latin, French and algebra exams were scorchers. He did best in his history but has been quite good all through. English standards seem to be so different from what I remember.

School for Susan is all play – so it seems. She sings all her tables, plays at reading and goes hopping merrily along. How pleased she was to be five – as if it were a special age. We made up a parody for her to sing, about Being Five. God how she did love her few and far between presents. She received some lovely books and spends hours over them. I think she enjoyed most her gift of a box of stationery as she is always trying to waylay mine to no avail! Now she writes letters to her heart's content.

Hilda spent yesterday and last night with us again. It is nice having her as a house guest as she fits in so well.

Luckily, while Susan has been ill there have been no sirens so as to take shelter and disturb her. Still the children now take raids just as so much passage of time under the dining table.

Last week I planted three apple trees, 2 dozen raspberry canes, a gooseberry bush, red currant and blackcurrant bushes and several dozen strawberry plants. As I planted them all with a beseeching prayer – let's hope this crop is terrific.

We've had our first snow and Lee went up to the Heath in high hopes of sledging but there wasn't sufficient.

We are all looking forward to Christmas. On my points ration I managed to get sufficient fruit for a cake, a pudding and some mincemeat. It's the first year I've let the children help and they have revelled in it.

Ronald joins me in love and best wishing, hoping you both are ever so well and cheery.

All my special love -

Your
Elisabeth

Letter Sixteen

8 Thornton Way
LONDON
N.W.11

April 5, 1944

To Mr. and Mrs. Lee Galt
125 Stanley Blvd.
Ardmore, Oklahoma, USA

Dear Mother and Papa

I had put aside tonight for writing to you and most opportunely a letter from both of you came this morning. It was good to read of you both so contented and happy. Lee like his letter and Susan too. They have heard so often about 'Francis' - a favourite story when the noise of the barrage increases in a raid. They love the story of Francis and Mother swimming together in Blue Hole. I'm glad you have a dog. I often think how you, Mother, would like our Dinah with her undying devotion and sincerity and how you, Papa, would like our Topsy with her undying energy.

What a splendid son and daughter, Monroe and Ethelyn are to you! I am proud of them and envy them their opportunity.

I am sure both of you look very spruce and grand, dressed in your new suits for Easter. I was just thinking today that this is the first Easter that there hasn't been a been a new outfit for at least one of us. But today we can patriotically say that we are 'making do'. However, I'll soon have to take Ronald in hand and force him to make use of our remaining coupons. Men's clothes seem so dear in coupon value and his wardrobe is at a low threadbare ebb with shirts, suits, underwear and coats very low!

However our thoughts today seem to turn to the suspense of the moment which is expected to break at Easter. Some of us know but it is so magnetically in the air we can talk of nothing else. The Second Front is At Hand. So long have we waited for this final thrust and sacrifice. May we grit our teeth the harder and plunge through successfully.

We have been practically raid-free this past week, a pleasant fact which coupled with the fragrant arrival of

Spring makes the world a joy to behold. I wish you could see the gardens behind, into which our own garden enters. The grass paths are bordered by a stretch several hundred feet long, of masses of daffodils. The many species of fruit trees are just coming out. It takes one's breath away with its ecstatic loveliness.

Last Saturday Col. Breedlove, who had phoned the previous day, came to spend the evening and night with us. He's a grand companion and it was a pleasure to have him, especially as he and Ronald seem to appreciate each other so. He said he intended to write to you after his visit so you should see us through his eyes as well! He brought – among other things – a packet of popcorn kernels which I have promised to pop for the children the first rainy day of the holidays. As they have never seen popcorn they are eagerly awaiting the new experience.

The second day of his visit was Lee's birthday. I've begged him to stay for Lee's afternoon party but he had to get back to his station. I think Lee enjoyed and considered his visit as one of the best of his birthday presents. Although it was wartime we seem to have accumulated for Lee quite a few useful presents: a new bicycle (really second-hand but in excellent condition) which is still a little too big but he can use his old one. We dared not risk passing up the chance of buying it when offered. Then there was his first fountain pen, a Morse Code set with an instruction game, a construction set of wood shapes, numerous books, cricket leg shields, and several oddments. The party itself was a huge success. His school friends were good pals and the competitive games went with a cheery spirit and swing. Susan is the only girl admitted into one of the games. So now Lee is officially nine and well ushered into his new year!

They both began their Easter holidays on Tuesday of this week. Lee sprang a surprise on us by finishing Top and first place in his class and being put up to a higher form (Grades are called forms, and instead of a year's work the year is divided into three terms of 12 weeks each). This was very good as he had only two terms in the one form. There is no need to say he does enjoy school. Susan's report was just to the effect that her reading was quite good and her arithmetic was improving. One couldn't expect much more at the age of 5!

I am planning to make their holidays as interesting as possible with several treats: Kew Gardens (to see the bluebells and daffodils), the Zoo (to see all the new spring babies), a theatre or two, etc. However at present they are content to play in the swing Ronald has erected (someone gave us one but it had to be unearthed and reinstated) and revel in the freedom and their friends. Susan is very elated because our tortoise has at last emerged from its winter's sleep.

Ronald is fire watching in town on Saturday night, his fire-watching premises having been rendered safe again. He doesn't fire watch at his office building but an allied building which was recently badly shaken by blast. Now that it has been strengthened the game goes on!

A note from Helen Horner said her sister, Eve, is also in England. I am hoping they can both get leave together next time and have their reunion here. I wonder if they will grow to love England as much as I have. It's time to fix a cup of tea before bedtime so I'll say a fond goodnight, hoping and praying you both are well and happy. Our thoughts are ever with you.

Love from us all,
Your affectionate
Elisabeth

Letter Seventeen

8 Thornton Way
LONDON
N.W.11

April 16, 1944

To Mr. and Mrs. Lee Galt
125 Stanley Blvd.
Ardmore, Oklahoma, USA

Dear Mother and Papa

No news from you this week, so I am eagerly awaiting the coming posts. Here goes for our version of the present days. They seem joyous happy ones with the children enjoying their holidays to the fullest, spring sprinting here, and the earth bursting with life. Our garden is indeed a revelation to us, for although I had turned all the beds and thought I knew every inch, we have been unprepared for the array of bulbs and plants which have appeared. And in the gardens at the back and around the almond, peach and cherry are an inspiration to behold. The grass seems too bright a green to be true!! It's a lovely world.

And yet it is a world which is breathing with an off-beat - so intense is its pulse while waiting for the second Front. We have been told by wireless and newspaper so often we are anxious to find out really what we in the second line of the second front can contribute. Germany now gives May 10 as the date - and we as usual are waiting to see!

Today has been a full blown April day with showers amazing and an inspiring freshness. As a family we went to church, the children separating for their respective Sunday School classes. The Minister today was a visitor from Guildford with an inspired address on 'Motives', an ideal theme in these moving times.

We came home to complete our dinner preparations and then had dinner. As Ronald said "I would never believe we would have such delicious and satisfying food in the fifth year, of this Our War." We had Roast Beef (the week's full ration) with Yorkshire pudding, roast potatoes, brown gravy, green peas – followed by Gooseberry Fool with sliced oranges – then coffee while the children had milk! Our tummies groaned.

This afternoon we opened our puppet theatre in the upstairs nurseries. It's a marvellous theatre Ronald and Lee have made, with proper miniature stage, lighting and ridiculously agile puppets. There is even a horse whose antics as Lee manipulates him has us rocking with laughter. Mr. & Mrs. Schedler with their two children came to see the show and have tea. I also popped some popcorn (from Col. Breedlove) and all the children loved it, having never seen or eaten any before. What simple pleasures – and such appreciation!

Last week Mrs. Schedler and Ronald exchanged children again and on my day out I went in to town again, did some essential non-coupon shopping and when finished went to a matinee to see the stage play Uncle Harry with Michael Redgrave admirably done! I hope to take Lee in to see some Shakespeare before his school reopens. He should appreciate the costumes and scenery and the flow of words – even if he is young for the poetic appreciation.

I must stop and do some sewing. I am trying to salvage Susan some panties or knickers out of some old pajamas of mine. She's outgrown and worn out practically every pair she has! So I'll say a fond cheerio hoping you both are well and happy.

Love from us all,

Ever your own
Elisabeth

Letter Eighteen

8 Thornton Way
LONDON
N.W.11

May 8 1944

To Mr. and Mrs. Lee Galt
125 Stanley Blvd.
Ardmore, Oklahoma, USA

Dear Mother and Father

There was a letter from you last week, stating you both were well and fit. I hope you continue to be so, and that you are well into the beginning of an enjoyable summer.

All of us are very fit, but it's like sitting on a live volcano watching for it to erupt – this second front anticipation. "When if ever" - if the cry and accompanies the break of every day.

There is still other ecstatic news which has cast us on further emotional clouds. In fact we are soaring!! Ronald has had another honour and the family follows his footsteps upwards – and upwards. He has been asked to take up the position of Director of Housing for the City of Glasgow in Scotland. The final confirmation of the appointment is not due for another three weeks, but it's merely a matter of routine so we are led to believe. All of which means we will be breaking up our London home and establishing residence in Glasgow. Our hopes are high for finding a house with an acre or two of ground somewhere between Glasgow and the famous Lochs. It's supposed to be famous and beautiful country. It should take two or three months to wind up business arrangements here, so that will give the children time to finish their present school terms here. As there are excellent schools in Scotland we should be able to enter them in schools as good as the ones they are leaving. Naturally they are upset at leaving here but their sadness will soon be appeased.

It's a marvellous opportunity for Ronald, combining all his architectural ability and his administrative experience. It's a chance of a lifetime. The salary commences at £1500 per year which speaks for itself. We hope you approve!

I am enclosing some recent snaps which will show you how happy and healthy your English family is! Lee seemed to see fit to cut a face for fun in most of them – but regardless of that, you can see something of what they look like.

Susan had a holiday today so she and I went into town for the day to get her some shoes. We tried eight shops before we could find any. She is pleased we were successful. I'll leave a short space for Roanld to add a line.

A fond goodnight to you both, and a loving prayer for your safe keeping.

Always your,
Elisabeth

Dear Mother & Father

Betty has told you the news of our possible move to Scotland! I need not say how excited I am at the change it offers and hope that there is not any slip between the cup and the lip. However all should be well – it's the sort of job I've always wanted and although it means another move just after we have got nicely fixed up here, I hope that this will be the last and that we shall be able to establish a permanent home.

You would love your English grandchildren – they are a fine couple of kids – full of spirit and abounding in good humour and fun. They are both all that I ever dreamed of. Lee is such a manly yet sensitive little fellow and enjoys life to the full. Susan is a little girl now and has left baby days behind her. You would also be proud of Betty (or I should say Elisabeth). She is a marvellous mother and we all worship the ground she treads on. We have been married ten years next week – ten years full of joy and happiness in spite of war and all its horrors.

I want you to know how I feel about your daughter. She is all that I ever hoped for, the perfect wife in fact. I know too that she is happy in her home, family and husband. In fact I like to feel that we are an ideal family. May the day soon come when we can all visit you so that you can see our happiness for yourselves. There's so much more that I could say about all this but somehow it's difficult to put these sort of things on paper. Anyway I want you to know that I love your daughter much more now than I did ten years ago and shall continue to do so come hell or high water!

Don't think because I don't write often that I have forgotten you or Ardmore. Sometimes I think that am more homesick for Stanley Boulevard than Betty – if that's possible. We do enjoy your letters – you can't write too often – the whole family fairly eats them up when they arrive.

I hope that you enjoy the photos – they give you some idea of us and our home.

All my love
Ronald

Letter Nineteen

8 Thornton Way
LONDON
N.W.11

May 21, 1944

To Mr. and Mrs. Lee Galt
125 Stanley Blvd.
Ardmore, Oklahoma, USA

Dear Mother and Father

This week has brought the confirmation of Ronald's Glasgow appointment, and with such many letters and telegrams of congratulations. Funnily enough the reporters released the news to the Scotch and Northern papers before Ronald had a chance to receive official notification. Such led to some amusement as well as embarrassment. However, it all seems a fact now which will mature in the very near future. He is giving notice here in London on June 1st which means the month's notice will take us into the first few days in July, when we should be on our way North.

Now that they have had time to recover from the sudden stun of the possibilities, we are all – Lee included – looking forward to the move. It will indeed be a new life! At first Lee couldn't bear to think of leaving his London school and friends. He's easier now and able to joke about it.

Speaking of Lee he was sent home from school on Friday with a mild case of German measles, which is so insignificant it could almost be passed by. As Susan has had it and Lee's case is so mild, she hasn't been placed in quarantine. Today she took place in a big pageant at the Church – Salute to China and did her part with great serenity and decorum. Lee was distressed to miss it – but he and Ronald held a checkers tournament and somewhat appeased his loss.
Before we go we plan to have a Family party on Sunday afternoon to say farewell to all Ronald's London relatives – not all exactly – but about 25 of them. We hope Mother Bradbury will come up for it. We have decided we'll see far more of Mother and Father when we live in Scotland, because of Father's fishing up there.

Summer must be coming as I have had my first attack of hay fever from all the May trees which are now heavy in blossom. Roses are due to burst this week as well – so I'll have a 'proper do'. Scotland is supposed to be gentle to hay fever addicts.

This past week we had a sleeping visit from Harry Middleton, one of our ex-S Shields friends now on the R.A.F. ground staff. He hadn't seen our London home and was pleased to find us so settled and happy. As the confirmation hadn't yet come through we couldn't tell him it was of short duration.

Each day when we awake we ask "Is it today" - and yet the Second-Front Blow hasn't fallen yet. Perhaps this prolonged expectancy has psychological value against the enemy – but we ourselves want the task to begin sooner!

I had a letter from D. Gifford Hart saying she was resuming summer residence in Montreal. She is sending another box of used clothing – all of which helps. She has been kind and thoughtful in these 'tight' years.

In sorting out old photographs we came across one of Uncle Jim. Where is he now and how is he? Papa said Leonard was doing nicely – what is his job now? Do give him and Mary our regards.

It's blackout time so I must close and put out the drawing shadows. I hope you both are well and happy. Let our love be with you, close and dear, always.

Your affectionate
Elisabeth

Letter Twenty

8 Thornton Way
June 18 1944

Dear Mother and Papa:

Perhaps I have been lax in the last ten days in getting off my weekly letter to you, but these have been most moving times. One seems to feel so much that words seem so inadequate to express all that is experienced. What was so long awaited came as you know at the crucial D Day. We awoke here in London, sensing there was something in the air. Lee had come into our bedroom about six-thirty and woke to ask if he could get dressed and go out. "There is such air traffic that I want to count the planes and recognise them." When he came back in about fifteen minutes to say that he had counted 264 in about ten minutes, we both agreed that something was afoot. The eight o'clock news gave us little information except what the enemy reported to be happening, but we had been so used to their stories that we would not let ourselves believe their gist of their work and words. Then before ten o'clock the official news came. The rest were at school and at the office, when I heard it alone. I did my house work with tears streaming down my face and my throat choked with emotion. I could not say why I cried, but I know that the prayers that were in my heart were prayers of both joy and sorrow. Later in the morning I had shopping to do which meant numerous queues. We housewives stood practically mute, forgetting to discuss what were the possibilities of the day's market. When one woman joined the green grocery queue, and remarked to the lady in front of her, "Isn't it exciting?" the lady who was serving in the shop squelched her with, "How can you say it is exciting when you see the faces of the other women here. They are all living and breathing with every moment passing until we know our foothold has been established. The excited woman held her tongue further. By that time she realised that the silence of that group of women was a sign of their suffering and experiencing of all that was going on across the channel.

And the news since then has been steadily good. We have watched the military traffic returning with empty trailers, etc. those which had gone by so laden not so long before. The air cover which has gone over and which we have been able to see from here has been stupendous night and day. The organisation of it is beyond imagination.

That was over ten days ago and we breathe more freely now. But other things have been happening as well. One night last week we had the first 'alert' in about eight weeks. As I was taking the children to the shelter on a clear moonlight night, Susan, who had just wakened sufficiently to know she was awake, said, "Oh, look at the red balloon in the sky." I looked and far in the distance from where the guns were roaring there floated a red, glowing ball high in the sky. Suddenly it just wasn't there anymore. The next day Ronald came home with the story that someone had told him a pilot-less plane had landed the night this happened. Such was the beginning of the intimation of what had really crystalized three nights ago. As it happened Helen Hornor was spending the night with us and we had all just gone to bed when the siren sounded. I knocked on her door and asked her if she wanted to go into the shelter with us if the guns started. She said, "Sure I'll come." The guns started and we assembled in the shelter in the back garden. The children were so thrilled with Helen's experiencing a raid with them, that they didn't go to sleep as they usually do, but we had what they call a shelter party. We told stories, and when the roar got very loud one of the grown-ups would start a loud rollicking song to drown the outside noise. Somehow there was a feeling that this raid was 'different'. We didn't know just how but we all commented on the fact, each noting some unusual detail: there was no thrilling uplift of the speedy sound of our fighters; the barrage seemed more directed and not an all-inclusive one; the sound of the enemy plane had a different note, sort of an oily, greasy sound – and then no noise at all. We generally began to wonder still further when the hours dragged on and the children grew tired of even the 'shelter party', and said they were going to sleep. The barrage all the time was continuous, and it steadily grew into the longest stay we had ever had in the shelter. Helen tried to sleep in her chair and when the sounds drifted further afield she said she was going to risk getting some sleep in a proper bed. Ronald, too, succumbed, but I swore I would stick it out until the all clear went as the children were sleeping soundly. At about seven I walked them into the house still asleep although the all clear had not gone. Seemingly, the siren gadget had broken but we knew in our hearts something new was abroad. The eight o'clock news gave us no intimation of what it was, so, since the gun noises were now distant ones, the children went to school, Ronald to work and I carried Helen her breakfast in bed. She deserved her ly-in! About nine-thirty the all-clear went and we all said that was that. I mounted my bike to do some shopping for some fish as there was no meat in view. While out shopping again the wail began, the first daylight alert London had had in so long. This went off and on, with dog-fights, guns, and a certain strangeness until the one o'clock news informed us that pilot less aircraft had been used against Southern England. Then we understood the previous red ball in the sky, the oily sound, the cessation of the engine before the explosion. It was like the illness of a child when, before the doctor comes to diagnose the case, one imagines so much. Then, when he does come and you know 'what is what' your relief at knowing counterbalances the suddenness of the illness. When we knew just what was happening we all took it in our stride as we do with so many things these days. However, it has been a deep broad stride this time, for the alert and all-clear are so steadily in use that it is even tiresome to ask: "How many alerts is that today?" We have spent the last two nights in the shelter, having converted it into sleeping berths for us all and spending the whole night there, letting it make little difference to us. We all go about our work and our play and if one hears that oily sound and sees the put-puts in the sky one knows to seek shelter. Lee and Susan are becoming quite good air-raid wardens. Yesterday we had Barbara (who came back from America only two weeks ago) here with her little girl who is experiencing raids for the first time. It is unfortunate because her morale and stamina is not built up as that of English children who have grown into it. It is no longer a danger but just one of those things in life: like not knowing what a banana looks like. As I write this it is the first breathing period we have had with a warning since it began – yet it seems to have made little difference to our lives, except those unfortunate ones whose homes were unlucky.

Now for other news: we had our large family tea party last Sunday with twenty one here for tea and ten staying on for supper. It was a jolly crew and all very grateful to be having a family reunion in war-time. I had saved for weeks to be able to cater for them, and somehow the food was even more than adequate, of an almost pre-war standard. Uncle Percy gave a splendid toast to Ronald on his new appointment.

We sold our hens and hen-house last weekend having inserted an ad in the local paper. We had almost 35 enquiries and we sold them immediately. We shall get reinstated with fowls again when we are settled up there.

It was good to have Helen H. with us again. I had intended writing to Kathryn or Mr. Hornor after her visit, to let them in on our doings (no comma) but, as I have written so long and fully to you, perhaps you could let them see this and save duplication. She did enjoy her day around 'a house' and thrilled at having on a house frock. She spent most of the afternoon curled up in a chair reading some of my books of poetry. She seems very much in love with the young Ft. Worth fellow she got engaged to in Africa and from his letters, he must be a splendid fellow.

As we shall be leaving here in the first week or so of July, Ronald advises that you address future letters as follows until we are established in Glasgow:

Address the letter as follows:
Personal

Dr. R. Bradbury
Director of Housing
The Corporation of Glasgow Housing Department
20 Trongate, Glasgow C.1. Scotland

You can tell anyone in Ardmore likely to write to use this address, as it will ease up the redirection of any letters here.

I do hope that both of you are fit and well and that the summer is being kind to you. How goes the garden and the hens; do they lay well? The children send their special love. All our love and keep happy.

Your own,
Elisabeth

Not forgetting your own Ronald also.

Letter Twenty-One

8 Thornton Way
LONDON
N.W.11

August 26 1944

To Mr. and Mrs. Lee Galt
125 Stanley Blvd.
Ardmore, Oklahoma, USA

EXAMINER NUMBER 5261

Dear Mother and Papa

It seems a long time since there was a letter from you but I trust you both are in good health and spirit. The four of us are likewise fine especially as we seem to be getting more settled. Ronald is now deeply embedded in his job and loving every busy moment of it. Lee and Susan are admitted and outfitted for their new schools and await for opening day on Sept. 5. We have finally found a house, one which the Corporation had requisitioned for Welfare Work and which we are renting until one that fits our dream ideal comes into the market.

We are really very lucky as it is a large, Redstone mansion on a hilly ridge that commands good views of the Clyde and the distant hills. It's in a very pleasant suburb of Glasgow and within easy reach of all parts of the City. Lee has a long tram or bus ride to his school but he is rather looking forward to it. Susan is just two blocks above her school. Maxwell Park with lovely gardens, yachting pond, tennis courts, swings, etc. is just at hand as well. We hope to move in in about 10 days or two weeks. The new address will be:
Bradbury
38 Sutherland Avenue
Pollockshields
Glasgow.

Sunday last we took a day's trip first to Garnock then across by steamer to Dunoon where the children went bathing in the sea. They loved the steamer ride although it only took 25 min.

We are making another visit to Edinburgh tomorrow, when Ronald is to play godfather to John Walkden's 3rd son. Susan is looking forward to the christening service. She wants to know if she can take your new nigger doll to be christened at the same time.

This afternoon I took Lee and Susan out to see Dinah and Topsy who are being boarded at the house of one of Ronald's secretaries. Topsy had had her third litter of pups four days ago and was feeling a bit sorry for herself as they had been drowned seeing her foster-mistress couldn't look after so many. They were glad to see us and begged so hard to come back with us.

The food situation in Scotland seems to be easier than in England, or perhaps it's because a Hotel can cater better than a private family. We seem to have ample meat, chickens, fresh salmon, tomatoes, fruit, etc.

Everyone is highly elated and overjoyed at the big news coming from France and all over the continent. What sweeping successes! There seems to have been even a lull in the flying-bombs on Southern England. If only London could have a rest! It's been hectic lately according to reports from our friends! I am glad we have the children away. Some nights even now I awake and find myself listening. It's hard to realize such tense endurance is over for us. I only hope it won't be too long for all the others there.

Give our love to all the family and I hope they have all had a splendid summer.

Love and kisses to both of you.
Ever your,
Elisabeth

Letter Twenty-Two

Moray Lodge
25 Newark Drive
Pollockshields
Glasgow.

November 8 1944

To Mr. and Mrs. Lee Galt
125 Stanley Blvd.
Ardmore, Oklahoma, USA

Dear Mother and Papa

Your letter arrived today with the clipping of Papa's squirrel shooting. I think it's marvellous that you're able to call forth such a press notice. It's a tribute to your stamina and your character. Both your letters were most cheery even though you referred to 'too many birthdays'. I only wish I had so many notable ones to my credit. It makes me warm and pleased inside to read that you are so well off and free from worries. That alone is a feat of which to be proud.

Mother you seem so delighted with Ethelyn's new addition, and I am overjoyed. It will give not only Monroe and Ethelyn a new interest in life – but also you too. I will never forget the months before Barry's birth and recall one day when I dusted and tidied up for Ethelyn in the little house next to Mildred's. How many, long years ago that was.

Yes – we are now fully settled in our home although only three weeks since we entered. The house now seems to belong to us as well as we to it. We have our first house guests, Mother and Father Bradbury who have come for 2½ weeks. Father B. has promised to write you a long letter relating to our new life, when he returns to Taxal Gate. They both have aged considerably, really more than their years I feel, although Father B. has shaken off the terrible depression he has harboured for the last two years. He is now jovial again – and says his change of heart came with Ronald's appointment.

Ronald is off tomorrow for a trip around England: Hull, London, Coventry to survey new types of houses. There is a committee of three going so it should prove a very invigorating trip. Mother and Father Bradbury are remaining until his return a week from hence.

Susan and Lee are in fine fettle although Susan has had a cold which she nursed in bed for two days, mainly because she wanted to be a queen in her lovely new bedroom with Grandma paying tribute by her side. They have spent hours reading, sewing (Susan made a small coat for one of her toy dogs – complete with pocket for handkerchiefs) knitting, and chatting. Mother B. enjoyed her days as much as Susan.

There is still so much to do to the house with odd jobs. Two workmen have been here all day fitting gas fires in the dining room and study to replace coal fires, the fuel for which our allotment does not cater. We are debating whether to have a gas fire inserted in the lounge upstairs to save labour and fuel in war time – yet one does hate to give up the intimate glow of a coal fire.

The Roosevelt election results are coming flooding in and Ronald and I are delighted that he is again returned. We had talked to so many Republican US visitors to Glasgow that we wondered how much to believe. More power and strength – and continued health to him!

I must write letters this week especially to Mildred whose second parcel arrived practically the day we moved. Since these I've hardly had a moment. I have a very good girl who comes twice a week to do my heavy chores which is a help after having had no one in London for so long. When labour restrictions are relaxed Glasgow should be swarming with domestic help – but war requirements are still foremost.

It snowed today in a shower of rain and the children look forward to the winter here where there should be good sledging, skating and winter sports. They both are growing so fast. I think I like them this age best of all – they are such companions.

Do keep care of yourselves. Lee says he'll write this weekend. Love from us all.

Ever your,
Elisabeth

Dear Father & Mother,

We were pleased to have Father's letter today enclosing the cutting about his squirrel shooting exploits. Great stuff, Father. I only wish I could join you on one of your jaunts for another lesson in shooting. However, maybe after the war we will have another expedition together – Here's hoping anyway!

I too feel miserable that I have not been able to send Betty over to see you again – I had planned to do so, as promised in 1939, but the war was so imminent that it was best policy to keep her here. I do hope both of you realise that it's not my fault that it has been so long since she came to see you. Would that I could have sent her both for your sakes and hers. She is very brave about separation from her loved ones and keeps her chin up most of the time. However, when a specially good letter comes from you, tears sometimes dim her eyes as she thinks about you and I do my best to comfort her. I feel so helpless about it but I do appreciate the great sacrifice that both you and she have made by letting her live here in England, and in consequence I do my best to make and keep her happy. I believe she is really happy now that she has a home of her own again, which she can enjoy with her two adorable children. You would love Lee & Susan.

I hope to send some more snaps soon. Films however are so difficult to get but now I've managed to promise one so let's hope they turn out well.

My parents are staying for a few days with us as our first guests – I wish it could have been you two instead! However, they are enjoying their stay, and the children and we are finding them good fun too.

Sometime I hope to get time to sit down to write you a really detailed account of your daughter who has developed into a really gracious and mature woman, very capable as a housewife, perfect as a mother whom the children worship, and ideal as a mate and companion for me. Of course we have our little misunderstanding occasionally but they are only ripples on the surface and the deep, deep pool of our love remains calm, serene and ever deepening as the years roll by.

Of course, I know that I am an awkward cuss to live with but she is so patient and understanding, and looks after me marvellously well! Thank you for giving her to me – a good wife is a pearl without price and she is the best of them all ------ I could write like this for hours but even I think mere words could not really convey what my feelings really are, about Betty. I feel very humble when I think how lucky I have been to have her.

We do think and talk about you a lot so that you are really with us although so many thousand miles away. Write often we love your letters so –

Ever your loving son,
Ronald

Letter Twenty-Three

Moray Lodge
25 Newark Drive
Pollockshields
Glasgow. S.1
Tel. Pollok 0112

January 16, 1945

To Mrs. Cecil Baker
1037 McLeish Avenue
Ardmore,
Oklahoma, USA

Dear Mildred and Eleanor

I am writing this to both of you so I won't repeat myself in two separate letters and thereby weary you.

Needless to say, my epistle is born with the arrival of your parcel which has just arrived. We feel so lucky with such gifts and revel in their use. Susan has devoured most of the hard sweets and wishes the cardboard container were like the old lady's pen-pot which refilled itself in use. Lee has cornered the popcorn and is issuing it out for special treats. He's such a hoarder we are wondering when he will make his first release. The sweaters are a great success and very needed as the children have elbowed practically all their sweaters. The colours are just what each wanted. The banana flakes were quite a novel surprise and I look forward to using them. So thanks so much. You have filled our hearts and our hands.

We had a good holiday, this first Christmas and New Year celebrated in Scotland. Here the former is no holiday but the latter is a double day holiday. Being English in Scotland we celebrated both. Schools here have 2½ weeks holiday and the children crammed them to the fill! They are again making new sets of friends.

House and home moving has the drawback for children in that they leave their world of friends behind them. Both Lee and Susan felt this keenly this time. Language is another element involved. They imitate so quickly that they assimilate whatever accent is at hand. Susan is pure Scottish brogue now with 'aachs and 'wees' peppered through her speech. However, Lee being older has still hung on to his B.B.C. London England.

I thought back some 25 years today to a Sunday afternoon when Mildred cut off my long braids and Mother cried. Susan has begged so hard to have her hair cut that today I took the bull by the horns and had it done before I weakened. Ronald almost wept. It changes her so – but she's far prettier. Her front teeth are now coming in so she has hopes.

They have both taken to the Scottish Sunday Schools and swear by their Sunday afternoons at the 'kirk'.

The winter here has been very cold but with hardly any snow which seems strange since England has had so much recently. The houses here are big, spacious and lofty – and heat with rationing and hold-ups is a bit scanty. We rarely ever use our grand lounge because we can't manage fires in both the children's study and the lounge.

What has ever happened to your Peke? Dinah, our pug and Topsy are still going strong alongside of Tigger, our cat. What joy the kids get out of them all.

I do hope you, and yours are well and happy and that the none too distant peace returns your businesses, etc. to normal.

Love from us all and thanks again.
Sis

Letter Twenty-Four

>Moray Lodge
>25 Newark Drive
>Pollockshields
>Glasgow. S.1
>Tel. Pollock 0112
>
>January 28, 1945

To Mrs. Cecil Baker
1037 McLeish Avenue
Ardmore,
Oklahoma, USA

Dear Mildred

Alas, my desire to thank you for your Christmas parcels made me answer too soon, for a further one has arrived – so here goes again.

What a blessing they have been! The food parcel was relished! We were having a tea party the day after the popcorn one arrived so the whole party trouped into the kitchen and popped some.

I wish you could have seen the consternation on the faces of both parents and children. The pecans were indeed a treat as well, and the jello seems too good to be true. Of course the high peak was the hose for the family. Lee's been begging so hard for Cub socks but I didn't have coupons to spare for extra-necessities. You can imagine how pleased he is. He says he'll be a better Cub now. Each week when I darn Ronald's woollen socks I swear they won't stand another needleful so you can well appreciate how well yours filled the need. Being warm ones they were ideal for these days. As for my hose, life seems very bright again – as I was beginning to wonder what was going to happen soon. Your present has answered my question. So thanks again, dear Mildred, for your gifts. They were grand in deed and thought.

This past week has been a curious one with intense cold, frost, ice and snow – little fuel – potato famine – stoppage of milk delivery – and frozen pipes. There's a laugh in it all, however – if only one can see through the ice!

Now that we have a maid again, it means our evenings are not so restricted. Ronald and I saw a very good production of Hedda Gabler, one of Ronald's favourites. The casting was excellent! Hedda, herself, couldn't have been better. Glasgow is very theatre conscious as so many plays open here prior to either London or provincial runs.

I think I told you Lee is taking Scottish country dancing at school. As I have found out through experience and also through watching Highland regiments give exhibitions – it takes 'toughies' to do the Scottish dances. You should see Lee practising in our big kitchen – pretending to do a real sword dance. Susan's quite good at the polka. She had us weak with laughter at tea last night when she took off an opera singer and dancer! We do like her with her hair cut and she adores it!

Take half an hour off some day and write to us, giving us all the news of you, Cecil and the young married ladies. It is an under-statement to say we are hungry for your tid-bits.

Love to you and Cecil
affectionately
Sis

Letter Twenty-Five

25 Newark Drive
Glasgow, S.1
May 12, 1945

Dear Mother and Papa:

It seems another age and even another world since last I wrote, for then it was full war and now it is peace in the European Theatre. Although we know that the battle is only half won and the Japs can be jolly awkward, you have no idea of the light-hearted feeling that accompanies our knowledge that the war on this side means no more bloodshed and no more danger. We have difficulty in realising that it was almost six years. It is only when I look at Susan who is a strapping young lady now and then think of her as a small babe in arms, that it becomes evident just how long six years can be. To measure the length of a war by your child's life may be crude but it brings the essence of the idea home.

Of course the events of the week before peace – or VE – day was declared, everyone knew it was the end and each and every one hung around the wireless as if his life depended upon it. But how different to be waiting for peace instead of waiting for war as we awaited Chamberlain six years ago. It is no mitigation of the fact to say that Britain went wild when the two days of victory were celebrated. Flags appeared from every house, mansion and close as well. Everyone stopped work and tried to see just how much pleasure, that had been bottled up for six years, could be expressed in two days. Crowds swarmed the city streets, choking the squares. Special programs of thanksgiving, dancing, etc. occupied the swelling crowd for hours until the night found its way into the morning. Perhaps Ronald and I were more sober in spirit than the rest, but we were nonetheless grateful that it is over for this side. How unscathed we have come out it all, and how lucky we have been for all four of us to be together and to have house and chattel intact.

On the evening of VE Day we took the children to the church Thanksgiving Service. Even their eyes were wet as it was concluded with God Save the King. Home from the service we lighted a huge bonfire composed of all the rubbish that would not go for salvage. Then there was the

King's speech after which we put the children to bed, still too dazed to realise that war was really over for them. Later in the evening we had some friends in to help us crack our Victory bottle of champagne which we had saved since 1938. It was indeed a day to remember.

Actually, the cessations of hostilities will make little difference on our civilian lives: rations will continue and we are warned that our rations may even be cut for so many countries are hungrier than we, and there is much famine. Clothes and household goods will probably be rationed for another year or eighteen months but I don't mind. We have become so used to this rationed life and exist so happily upon it that I shall regret it's ever going.

I am eagerly awaiting news of the births of both Ethelyn and Mary Machen's babes. I do wish that I could see them. I hope all four of them are well and doing fine.

How glad I am that Mr. Blake came by to see you and give you first-hand knowledge of the Bradbury brigade in Glasgow. How well I remember the driving snow in which he visited us. I wish he were here now for Scotland is beautiful in her spring glory.

Today is Ronald's and my eleventh wedding anniversary and yet it seems like only yesterday that we were married. Today as also Lee's big sports day at his Academy, so the four of the family had lunch at a very grand restaurant in town, then went out to Lee's playing fields where the sports were held. I am sorry to say that Lee tried hard, but didn't carry off any honours. His laurels fall to him in the scholastic rather than the athletic field. Yet there was great fun and enjoyment on his part, and the day was quite an event.

Last night we entertained about fifteen of the Heads of Departments under Ronald as Director of Housing. I gave them a buffet supper, and the evening was a great success although it shook me to have Ronald addressed as 'The Director this' and the 'Director that' or 'Dr. Bradbury' here and 'Dr. Bradbury' there. His work as Director of Housing will be more onerous and essential now that the program is a present war and not a Post-war one.

All four of us are in good health and enjoying the glow of summer that has descended upon us. We have the hammock up for Susan. We have also made a four-hole golf course in the two front lawns and it is great fun.

I do hope that both of you are well and feeling in the best of spirit. Our thoughts are with you always, as is our love.

Your loving Elisabeth

Letter Twenty-Six

25 Newark Drive
Moray Lodge
Glasgow, S.L.

May 17, 1945

Dear Mildred:

In a letter from Mother this week there came news of Mary Machen's son's birth. How pleased I am that the event went off so soundly and well and that the son and heir is the thriving result. I am sure you are proud of your first grandchild and wish you and Cecil much pleasure and joy in its presence.

Your recent letter was full of interest and concern for us. I was glad to have your picture of Mother and Papa and only hope that now the spring and summer have come, it will find them better than in the winter months. Papa has been marvellous in his letter writing, and it does me good just to receive his letters.

Can you realise yet that the war in Europe is over? It seemed so sudden and yet it was expected for the preceding events had so clearly pointed out what was to happen. I have fully described the reaction to victory in Glasgow further in Mother's letter so I want not to repeat in case of boring you. The relief that intimate and near danger is over is immense, yet the problems of peace are going to be even so much harder than those of war. Then we fought the Germans, now we fight the wrong and selfishness that is in ourselves. Ronald is deep (mentally and physically) in his re-housing problem, the greatest that faces any man in Britain at this time. His shoulders are square and his head is screwed on right, for which I am indeed grateful for the solution and carrying out of his solution will take much turning and twisting of brain and brawn.

We are being strongly warned that the food situation is going to become much worse for the coming winter. Meat, sugar and butter rations are to be cut. It seems little enough as it is, but I am glad that it is big enough to cut to feed those millions in Europe who are so in want and hunger. Our garden here is a big one with wide, handsome lawns surrounded by deep borders which I have interspersed with vegetables among the already existing flowers.

We have also been told that clothes coupons will have to go further and last longer. The stress and strain on them at present is pretty severe but what has to be will be. I look with pleasant satisfaction on the many gifts that you have sent. What I would have done without your shoes both to Susan and me, I hate to think. Your Christmas stockings just about saved my legs and I am tending their possession with great care. You said they were not a sheer as you might desire, but they are grand compared to what is released here. Also with hose costing three coupons a pair, one can't afford them out of the coupon budget. Susan's dresses that I made out of the woollen green material and the checked taffeta that Mary sent are her prized possessions. I wish you could see her now. She is beautifully made with a straight well-formed body, much poise and grace and a colouring that shames peaches and cream. With her hair short now and curled, it frames her face with a fluffy prettiness. But it is her bright blue eyes that take the prize.

It is Lee's clothes that take all of his coupons and most of mine because being school uniforms you can neither make them nor substitute something else for them. His colours are gentian blue and grey and he looks very smart in his blazer and cap. Even though he gets better and bigger in size his features are still like those of the little boy that came to see you in '37. The freedom of the life here, travelling across this big city to his Academy by bus, train or underground – the association of the many types at his huge school have developed him into a fine lad. He is now a full scout although he is younger than the age limit and he is enjoying all that it entails. He was top of his form (class) last term and is making strong efforts to do so again. Yet he loves cricket, football, tennis and golf.

We are booked at a hotel at Cullen on the other side of Scotland for the last two weeks in July, when I hope to give them lots of swimming in the sea. Also, I am planning to start them going regularly to the indoor swimming baths here now that the warmer weather has come.

Ronald has taken up oil painting as his relaxation from housing and he is becoming amazingly good. He has just done a portrait of Lee which is not only definitely Lee but is definitely a good painting. Susan and Lee both have shots at the easel and oils and think they are as good as their father.

Susan is doing very well with her music, but I am afraid it gives little pleasure to Lee. I too have taken up my music again. It is needless to say how foolish I felt after a twenty year lapse but I am now enjoying it to the same extent that Ronald is his painting.

The basic ration of petrol is to be restored soon, and already Ronald is saying he must buy a car again. He has one for his work belonging to the city (a small working one housed near his offices) and he also has use of the big chauffeured city cars for official use – but yet he again has this home-car craving. The children have forgotten what having a car meant and so have I, although we had two at the start of the war. It is one of those things that we learned to do without so successfully that I have got out of the habit. I would miss the trams, buses and undergrounds!

Now that the war in this area is over we are thinking of our trip home. Because of the still mined seas and the Jap war which restricts shipping, etc. and the high costs of living and travelling, it would be impossible to think of taking all four of us home this year. We plan to do it next summer when the children and I shall spend about three months with you and Ronald will come for his month's holiday.

I wish that you could meet our maid, Mary. She is a grand type of Scottish girl and so smilingly conscientious and happy both in her work and with the children. She is so badly in need of clothes (underclothes, shoes – two sizes smaller than me) that I am doing my best to make my clothes stretch to both her and me. She is so appreciative. She recently said that she was not really happy until she came to us. That is why I am only too pleased to do anything for her in return, and her presence here has certainly made my life easier with this big house, garden and four of a family. Speaking of family leads me to the dogs who are both thriving into a grand old age. The cat, Tigger, tried to meet death by chewing and swallowing a ball of wool which stuck in her tummy and wouldn't either go up or come down. She was five days without any food, and finally I had forced so much liquid paraffin down her that it lubricated the wool and it passed on its way out. She had swallowed enough to make a small jumper. Oscar, our tortoise, which Lee brought all the way from London, has again awoken from his winter's sleep. When it is very wet we bring him indoors and he and Tigger sleep in a box together.

Do forgive the many mistakes in this ill-typed letter but there seem to be many distractions. I must close now to fetch some fish for tonight's dinner as there is still meat only for the weekend. Fish in Scotland is good; plenty of sole, halibut, whiting, cod and salmon if and when you can get it.

Give our love to Cecil and tell him that we hope all goes well with him. Is he still playing golf? He'll have to come to Scotland to have a golfing holiday over some of the famous courses here, where golf originated.

I hope the mother and son are going well and only wish that I could see them. We have sent them a special card under separate cover. Love to you all and thanks again for your grand letter. It did us all good.

Affectionately, Sis

Letter Twenty-Seven

Moray Lodge
25 Newark Drive
Pollockshields
Glasgow. S.1
Tel. Pollok 0112

May 30, 1945

125 Stanley Blvd.
Ardmore
Oklahoma, USA

Dear Mother and Papa

It has been about ten days or two weeks since last I heard from you and I am still eagerly awaiting the news of Ethelyn's new baby. How are Mary Machen and her son progressing? Do give my love both to Ethelyn and Mary Machen. I know they are happy in their new found joy.

Are you two keeping well now that summer has found its way to you? I was reassured to get your combined assurance that you both are as well as to be expected. Still I do wish I could see for myself. Can my letters do that for me?

Our brigade are fine and flourishing. I don't think I have ever seen the children in better health. They are looking forward to their summer holidays in six weeks' time at Cullen. I hope the bay there is as good as it is made out to be. We have made our back garden here into a play garden for the children, mostly Susan's crew, as Lee goes to the boating ponds, cricket fields, etc. Ronald made a sand pile out of rustic timber and cement, surrounded by a cement path. This, the swing and the hammock all have great support from the children. Susan has become quite expert on her big two wheel bicycle and the four of us go 'en famille' for nice long rides. Topsy and Dinah have seats on the carrier on the front of my bike. You can imagine the smiles we get as our brigade passes!

Susan has organised a Saturday morning class for two little boys age 3 and 4 and she puts them through their paces as if it were a proper kindergarten. Their Mothers think Susan is quite clever as their sons are really learning.

For a long time we have been asking Lee what he wants to be when he grows up. Until now he's always evaded the question by saying 'a chimney sweep' with a merry twinkle in his eye. The other day he said "I've decided what I want to be!" "What?" I asked expecting it to be a foreman chimney sweep as a joke. "A Minister" he said. He was so serious and went on in detail as to the why and wherefore of his decision. Time shall tell, of course, but over here one has to plan so far ahead. We are wondering whether to send him to a Public (Prep) School – boarding school of the Eton type – or to keep him at his Kelvinside Academy until he is ready for Oxford. Then the question of whether a boarding school in Scotland or England. It is indeed a question of study.

Last Friday Ronald was invited to sit on a Brains Trust at a meeting held at Linlithgow the birthplace of Mary Queen of Scots. We were highly entertained by the Provost (mayor) of the small town and shown over the Palace and Museum, to which we must take Lee with his great love of history. The Brains Trust was a great affair in the evening and Dr. Bradbury acquitted himself admirably along with a Head Master, a Psychiatrist, a Civil servant and two other dignitaries. I still marvel at the Scottish sense of humour.

This week Ronald is attending a Conference at Aberdeen where he is presenting a technical paper to the assembly. His hours here are so busy and so full, and impregnated with so much weight and worry I wonder at his endurance. However he seems to be growing and deepening with his job and his capacities are broadening. He will survive!

Last Sunday was the prize giving at the children's Sunday School, when the entire morning's service was given over to their session. Lee came away with two prizes, one for attendance and one for scholarship. Susan's looking forward to the day when she can really compete.

I have been busy sewing and sewing: remaking all Susan's summer dresses so they'll see her through this summer without spending her coupons which are so needed for other things for her. I made an artist's smock for Ronald when he does his oil painting – out of blackout material. Then a morning dress for Mary out of our old loose cover for a settee. My next job is to knit Lee some swimming trunks as he has outgrown his and they don't make them anymore – a luxury, not a necessity!

Our rations have been cut again this week. We are down to 3 oz. of bacon a week and one oz. of lard. Meat is down to 25 cents per week per person. Yet there are so many places without any meat or fats – we are really lucky.

Today is the day to collect our next ration books so I'm off to join the queue. Do keep care of yourselves and know our love is always with you.

Love from us four,
Your Elisabeth

Letter Twenty-Eight

Moray Lodge
25 Newark Drive
Glasgow, S.1
June 13, 1945

Dear Mother and Papa:

It seems almost as if I had had a visit from you as there was not only a long letter from Papa which arrived today but also one from Mary giving further news and views of all of it. It is needless to say how much we enjoyed both of them.

I am sorry that Mother was suffering from her teeth, but by now I am sure that they are all safely out and that she is proudly sporting her newly possessed dentures. It will be a relief to you, Mother; to think that that ordeal is behind you and that you need have no further teeth troubles.

Lee, Susan and I paid our periodic visits to the dentist this past week. Lee won't have me go with him, but makes an appointment to suit himself and some trivial remark passes from his lips as to the fact that the dentist did this and that. He takes it very matter of fact but Susan does not appreciate the drill although she is really very brave about it. She does all her worrying beforehand. I missed her soon after we came home from our appointment and eventually found her in the bathroom, which she had rigged out as a very efficient dentist's surgery. I regret to say that she had put each of her eighteen dolls through a very stiff course of treatment.

The reports on the new babies do sound superb. I know that you are revelling in your new granddaughter. She is lucky that she has you near her to be the doting grandmother. Is there any resemblance to Barry, and is he doing the big-brother act of the usual older brother? It is a shame that there is such a difference in their ages for the brother and sister companionship is a marvellous thing. It is so with Lee and Susan anyway: perhaps because they have so often been uprooted from their hosts of friends, at which times the constant companionship of each other is comforting.

I still get a great shock when I look at them and realise that no longer are they little girl and boy but big, growing children with strong, formative minds and a sense of what is right and wrong. Last Sunday the family of four took the train to Largs for the day and it was a heavenly day, with British summer at its softest and loveliest. I still think that the country around here is the nicest in the world. The sea comes in to meet the mountains at Largs and the blues, greens and greys have a fine combination. We found a sandy stretch of the beach where the children did their swimming and exploring among the rocks of a small island. Then we took a trip in a motor launch and were just lucky at that moment to sight the Queen Mary as she came steaming near. It was a lovely sight although she is now ocean grey instead of her former glistening colours. After the trip, we spotted some horses and ponies which were being let out on the sands; the children had turns on those. Further along the beach there was a huge Sunderland seaplane on observation, and beyond that there was one which had previously escaped from her moorings in a storm and had unfortunately broken up on the beach. Her whole insides were naked to view and it thrilled Lee to see the mechanisms so exposed. In the journey home on the train they were so tired that Lee fell asleep but Susan was resolved that she wouldn't succumb. It was funny to watch her winning struggle.

Britain is now in the midst of her pre-polling day campaign and it is an all-out struggle. Ronald and I have listened intently and studiously to all the political speeches by the three major parties, and it is indeed a revelation. The Conservatists at one end with the Labour at the opposite end, and the Liberals sitting nicely mid-way between. Some of the speeches have been excellent. The speech that Eisenhower gave after he was given the freedom of London has won heart-felt appreciation in the minds of all of us. What he said couldn't have been better said – or better thought. In many of the papers it was printed side by side with Lincoln's Gettysburg Address so you can see what high opinion it aroused.

I took Lee to see the film Wilson since he is so interested in both history and current events. We rarely take the children to the films, for there seems to be such little time left for that after all the rest they seem to want to do. We take them when there is something that they will especially enjoy and gain from. Lee sat entranced and learned much about American procedure in the way of residents. He was impressed that Wilson's second wife was a Galt.

You will be sorry to hear that Mary, the maid, is ill in the hospital with an appendix operation, but she is doing nicely. She collapsed a week ago today on her day out when she was visiting her mother and was operated on a few days later. Susan does miss her so, as they were such good pals. I am managing fine without her as it is now summer and there are no coal fires and extras such as that to worry about. She will be away until we come back from our holiday in July which should give her full time to recuperate.

Ronald is busy in the happy birth pangs of a book on the housing problem of Glasgow. It should arouse much comment and shake many people into the feeling of acute awareness that is necessary to bolster up his mammoth program. When he gets so saturated with housing that he eats and sleeps it, he takes time off and does an oil painting. He has just submitted one to the coming exhibition at the Glasgow Art Club, to which he has recently been elected a member. (a copy of the picture?) He is hoping that the picture will not let him down. I am sure that it shall do the opposite. He is looking amazingly fit and well at present although his cruel shoulder, which was cracked in the shelter at London, still gives him trouble. We are hoping in time that the wrongly knit bones will right themselves.

Letters from Mother and Father Bradbury do not find them too bright. Mother Bradbury complains of being so tired and, for one who has had the energy of ten women, this is indeed an ordeal. I thought the return of the basic petrol ration would cheer Father B. up, but I firmly believe it is the return of the basic meat ration that he is concerned about.

I am hoping to have some photographs made soon so that you can see the advanced stage of your grandchildren, but so far haven't been able to fit the time into our daily program. It must be done soon.

It is now time for Churchill's second campaign speech on the wireless so I shall sign off, hoping that you both are well and free from all aches and pains. Don't kid yourself that you are beyond letter writing Papa. You are doing better than ever. Keep care of yourselves and know that we are with you constantly. Love from us all, always.

Ever your affectionate,
Elisabeth

Letter Twenty-Nine

Moray Lodge
25 Newark Drive
Glasgow, S.1
July 15, 1945

Dear Mother and Papa:

I have two letters of yours to answer, and I sincerely apologise for not keeping pace with the one that came last week and the one that arrived yesterday. However, I am sure you understand when I say that Mary, the maid has been away until a few days ago with her appendix operation and I have had my hands full with the house, children, garden, shopping, fruit bottling etc. So here goes for a master attempt on a very rainy Sunday afternoon, which will make up for my lapse of two weeks.

First of all, let me say how sorry we are about the appearance and worry of the birth mark on the new baby. I am sure that by now all the treatment has been completed and that the results are showing themselves. Even if science wasn't so wonderful and effected so many marvellous cures, a small birth mark would be nothing to mar the baby's beauty. It might even prove a beauty spot and enhance her charm. Beauty spot or no beauty spot I do wish that we could see the young lady and add our praises to those of others. I am sure that Ethelyn and her family had a splendid visit and wish that I could drive the Atlantic as easily as she did the Texas miles.

How very nice of Mary to present you with another suit, Papa. I am sure you are the envy of all the other gentlemen and swish that we, too, might see you in all your splendour. If you have, as you say, so many Mother will have to do what I have done with one of Ronald's – get a good tailor to convert it into one for me. Turned and beautifully tailored, it looks as grand as any from Bond Street. I am glad that your clothes have never been rationed, for it is indeed a clever problem, sometimes too clever to solve.

s so excited about the coming holidays. We leave on Tuesday for Cullen. If you get out your map of Scotland you will find it up north on the other coast, beyond Inverness. Cullen is only a small village but it is supposed to have beautiful scenery, a wonderful beach, good tennis courts, a golf course – and all the things that lend themselves to a holiday from Housing. We are taking Lee's tent for putting up on the sands, the football, the tennis rackets, the golf clubs, the cricket bat, Ronald's paints and my knitting. However, none of us are looking forward to the train journey, as these last two weeks in Scotland are the official holiday period and everyone has taken to the rails since petrol rationing does not yet allow long distance travel. The queues that have assembled at all the big Glasgow stations this week have been a mile long – what waiting. The people are in peace-time holiday spirit but the railways are not yet able to cope with them.

The children have had two weeks of holiday from school already and they have enjoyed themselves. I have taken them to the swimming baths and tennis courts regularly, and the garden here is always full of their friends. Lee is doing a lot of reading; now plodding faithfully through Scott's Tales of a Grandfather, which was his school prize for being top of his form. Susan, on the other hand, is becoming quite domesticated. At my last pastry session she made some apple tarts which melted in your mouth and were quite professional to look upon. She has also become quite a little sewer and has made a presentable doll, mended all her dolls' clothes and tried her hand at knitting. She also spends a lot of time at the piano, making up tunes and words to accompany them. Somehow they always seem to harmonise.

Speaking of your gift of a squirrel, we had a very acceptable gift of a large salmon, just freshly caught and it was indeed a treat.

Our very old dog Dinah has not been too well as she had been suffering from bladder trouble. Ronald tries to prepare me by saying that she cannot last forever but, as I hated to think a long time ago that old Frances could ever pass on, so I hate to think of losing Dinah. She is as old as Lee but to me she is as young and beautiful as ever.

Thanks for the clipping, Mother, of Helen Horner's wedding. Either she never wrote or her letter never reached me, because your clipping was the first intimation we had that the love-birds (as Lee termed her and her fiancé when they visited us) were married.

I am sorry about the absurd behaviour of my typewriter in this letter but what it is doing is beyond my control and all my fiddling with it only seems to make it worse. After all, it too has had a long life and deserves a rest.

We will send you a line from Cullen so, until then, keep well and happy and have a lovely summer.

We all send our love and kisses.
Elisabeth

Letter Thirty

Grant Arms Hotel
Cullen
Banffshire

July 23, 1945

125 Stanley Blvd.
Ardmore
Oklahoma, USA

Dear Mother and Papa

From the above address you will see that we are high up in Scotland, in the middle of our holiday by the sea. I do wish you could see the country and scenery around here. It is rugged with unusual rock formations jutting out to sea, with long stretches of beach that has sand as fine as ground glass. There are many walks that lead you along winding shores, up stony cliffs and over windswept headlands. There is no need to say that the children are loving it. There is a protected harbour where they can swim or the wide stretch of beach where they can ride the breakers. There are long piers from which they can fish – mainly for plaice. Susan collected a whole tribe of jellyfish one day. One walk we took over a headland led the children by many exciting caves. Lee started collecting wildflowers and by the time we reached home he had 25 different varieties. On one deserted rocky shore there is a salmon fishery hut where you can order whole salmon to take home with you, bound fisherman-style in reeds.

Yesterday was Sunday and we all went to church at the lovely old church in Cullen House Grounds, where the Countess of Seafield lives. We have a pass for these grounds anytime and it's a revelation to see such a handsome, commanding castle (or house?) in such heavenly grounds.

Yesterday afternoon we joined some friends for a run along the coast to all the neighbouring fishing villages. Nearby at Buckie the entire fishing fleet has been on strike for over 10 days because of a revolt against government continued control of fish markets. It was a sight to see so many fishing trawlers, sailing boats, etc. crammed into one harbour.

We've brought our tennis and golf kit but so far the sea and scenery have had the strongest attraction. We are all looking better for the rest, the air and the change. The journey up here was not as long or tiresome as we expected. I saw Aberdeen for the first time. It's a fine, clean city.

I do hope this finds you both well and having a 'not too hot' summer. Have you got your new teeth, Mother and do they feel natural yet? It must have been an ordeal! We all send you our love and hope you both are smiling and happy.

Affectionately yours,
Elisabeth

Letter Thirty-One

Moray Lodge
25 Newark Drive
Pollokshields
Glasgow. S.1
Tel. Pollok 0112

Aug 7, 1945

Mrs. L. N. Cox
1007 McLish Avenue
Ardmore
Oklahoma
USA

Dear Mary

Your recent letter gave us much news and much pleasure. Your description of the new babies made me very anxious to see them. In you I am sure they have found the devoted auntie. We also liked your description of the New York trip and we relived many of our experiences there through your eyes. So sorry to have to disillusion you, but we were married not in The Little Church around the Corner but in the Cathedral of St. John the Divine. However, we attended many services in the former and did appreciate seeing the lovely colour picture of it.

Your parcel arrived many weeks after your letter, hence my delay in answering your letter. Mary, the maid, wishes me to express her sincere thanks for the shoes, which were an ideal fit and which she so greatly needed. They look very smart on her and she is getting steady wear out of them. I am making up the white material as two afternoon aprons, which she also needed as her present ones are almost in tatters.

The black dress fits me to perfection except a bit long and will give me much wear. With clothes coupons recently reduced an extra dress is a big item in making up a presentable wardrobe. The paisley dress will yield amply to treatment and I am looking forward to getting time to operate upon it. Thanks so much for your help and co-operation., It has been a great help.

The next thing on the agenda is a request for help in another form. Papa's last letter which arrived yesterday has again stressed upon Ronald's and my mind the fact that I should get home as soon as possible to see him and Mother. As Mildred said in a recent letter, "Papa is getting no younger." Under present circumstances: priority, high income tax, etc., it would be impossible to get the whole family of us over this year or even the early part of next year. I could get priority on compassionate grounds if I had a doctor's statement from his doctor stressing the necessity of my seeing him soon. I do not want to ask Mother to get this for me as it might raise undue hopes if anything fell through. Therefore, could you get such a statement from his Doctor on his headed paper and I'll see what can be done with it from this end.

We are hoping to get a 'pull' on the Donaldson Line which would enable me to come without any bother and would also land me in Galveston and hence save the long N.Y. Journey. If things did mature I would have only a very short time at home because the family here would be without anybody in my stead. Ronald's parents are both 'ailing' and couldn't cope with this big household. We both say that my Father will outlive his Father.

Such then are the tentative plans and I'll leave it in your hands to get the Doctor's statement. Please don't mention it to Mother or Papa, for the plan might easily not mature as arranged and would hence cause undue worry or excitement.

In my recent letters to Mother I gave full reports of our splendid holiday at Cullen. It was delightful with the most beautiful rugged scenery and quaint fishing atmosphere. The sea straight from Iceland was bitterly cold but the children bathed just the same.

Ronald is as busy as ever – even more so! Yesterday he showed the New York Housing Mission our Glasgow schemes. His job is really staggering!

The children are both very fit and very happy – and oh, so grown up now. They are now the ideal companions and Ronald and I are revelling in them.

Britain is shaken by the news of the atomic bomb. What a breath-taking discovery. One trembles at its possibilities. The Labour victory has been overwhelming and it's as if a new breath of political life had come. Churchill is just as revered but his party has lost its grip.

    Do give my regards to Machen and Mr. Cox. Keep all our love – and special auntie kisses from the children.

Love,
Sis

Letter Thirty-Two

Moray Lodge
25 Newark Drive
Pollokshields
Glasgow. S.1
Tel: Pollok 0112

August 29,1945

To Mr. and Mrs. Lee Galt
125 Stanley Blvd.
Ardmore,
Oklahoma, USA

Dear Mother and Papa

It seems a long time since there was any letter from you, so I trust your delay has been due to too hot weather and to nothing more serious. We do like to get Papa's letters and wish you, Mother dear, would send us a nice long one as well. We may be far away but you both are nearer and dearer to us than ever.

We have Ronald's auntie and uncle Percy Symmons from London with us for two weeks and we all are enjoying their visit immensely. Uncle Percy retired last year as Chief Surveyor of the London County Council so he has been doubly interested in the layout and erection of all of Ronald's schemes.

We seem to have 'gone places and done things' with their being here or perhaps it is that we finally feel peace is here and we can at last relax. Having a car again makes life so much easier and enjoyable. It's been too good to be true to be able to get into the country or to the seaside without having to queue for a bus or a train.

Susan doesn't remember ever having had a car before so you can imagine how thrilled she is at the experience.

Poor Dinah, our faithful and devoted pug for over ten years was gently put to sleep today. It was the kindest thing to do as she was suffering so. Her womb, which had been sorely taxed by her one and only litter of pups (the father was a mongrel many times larger than Dinah) played itself out – first by great flooding and then infectious pus. The vet said he could operate but as she had had two heart attacks recently he said she wouldn't live through an operation. It was a sad end to such a glorious dog! Susan, Lee and I have wept all day. Even Topsy and her six frolicking pups don't seem to cheer us. However we will get over it!

Topsy's pups are just at the right age for cuteness now. As pert, saucy and gnawing as possible. We had them in the sun today – lapping up their bread and milk. Six busy souls with their tails pointed to heaven!

We've taken auntie and uncle to two theatres: 'The Hasty Heart', the Burma war play and 'Hi Caledonia', a Scottish revue with lots of Highland dash. We took the children with us to this latter one and Susan is determined to learn the sword dance at once – and Lee as determined to buy a pair of bagpipes.

With the cessation of land-lease (which I personally think should end now the Jap war is over and America no longer needs what we could leave here) we in Britain face the most depressing winter of the war years. Our food rations (especially of meat, bacon, fat, cheese and butter) is the lowest it ever has been and is predicted to go lower. Our clothes ration has been cut – or rather has to extend further, with no chance to replace anything yet. I think we are laughing it off – we're so glad it's really peace – and so glad that we haven't the desperation and destruction that is on the Continent. We have much for which we can be thankful.

The pictures which we took on our Cullen holiday and later here at Moray Lodge are enclosed. I do hope they show you something of us as we are today.

Lee and Susan are due to resume their schools next week and are so looking forward to it although they have had a grand holiday.

The children send you special greetings and kisses and Ronald and I, our deepest love.

Affectionately yours,
Elisabeth

Letter Thirty-Three

Moray Lodge
25 Newark Drive

Sept. 14, 1945

Dear Mother and Papa:

The morning lies before me with many things crying out to be done, but first of all a long letter to you. The children are both away at school now, having begun the autumn session last week. They were so anxious to be again in harness that on the first day they were awake and dressed by six, demanding their breakfast. The night before there was much ado about sharpening pencils, collecting materials, etc. Lee is first out of the house at a quarter to eight each morning, as it takes him about forty-five minutes to cross Glasgow to reach Kelvinside Academy. He was offered a place in a friend's car which will go every morning much later now that petrol rationing has been restored, but Lee declined saying that he would rather have the fun of the buses, the underground and the tramcars. Ronald also bought him a season ticket on the train (which takes him half the distance), so he considers himself quite a grown man now. I will say that the travelling and knocking about this big city has given him an assurance and confidence that few boys of his age acquire.

Susan doesn't leave home for her school until an hour later as it is only a ten minute walk down Newark Drive, where it lies by Maxwell Park. She is begging so hard to be allowed to ride her bike to school but I still think she is a bit young. I had to sacrifice three of her clothing coupons for a school tie and school scarf, for which she begged so hard. Last year I had made her make do with an old one of Lee's which was almost the same colour, but this year she maintains that she is a proper school girl and that she has to have the proper uniform. She looks about like a girl of nine instead of six and is as happy as the day is long.

Last Sunday we were invited as a family to the country home of our solicitor who lives at East Kilbride, a lovely village not far from Glasgow. The house and estate has been in his family for six generations, but only he and his older sister are living there now. They have only a housekeeper where before they had six servants – yet the place looks perfect. There was much of interest for us all as she had been a superb painter in her prime, and he has travelled far and wide, collecting curios as he went. The thing that amused Lee most of all, however, was an object that looked like a fossilized stomach of a horse, and which in fact was a huge dust ball which had collected and grown in the tummy of one of their riding mares, until it had grown so large that it killed the horse. This fascinated Lee ... this and all the swords, armour, etc. of the fifty different countries represented. Susan liked the collection of teapots that the Miss Strang had, all belonging to six generations of her family. We had afternoon tea in the garden, and later dinner in the massive dining room. I thought at first the children would be over faced with it all, but they were the life and soul of the party – until Susan said she was ready to go to bed as it was past her bedtime at 7:15.

Ronald's Aunt and Uncle from London left last week after their two week stay and we did enjoy them. Auntie had stayed on a few days longer than Uncle as he had to get back to some meetings. She did enjoy her rest, her first after the six hectic war years spent in London. She had earned her breakfast in bed. The night before she left we had a dinner party and then the theatre (Evelyn Laye in the Three Waltzes) and she did enjoy it.

The day after Auntie left Ronald played official host to Lord Airley from Birmingham who had come to see him on business, while I had to play unofficial hostess to Lady Airley who had accompanied ;them. I found them both charming and gracious; not in the least affected. Ronald has to go to London in Oct. and they are begging me to come that far with him and have a few days with them. It always amuses and amazes me to see with what deference, respect and admiration these 'top-notchers' in Building, Labour and Architecture treat Ronald. They hang upon his every word and court his every whim. Nice compliments in themselves!

There is a feel of winter in the air and one begins to think of clothing and fuel. The clothing coupon continuance and cut has left us all aghast, wondering how things will possibly last for another year or eighteen months. There are so many things that want replacement that it leaves nothing for the little ones (hose, stockings, handkerchiefs, vests, etc.) or the other way round. Yet we see the reason of the continuance and look forward to better days. We are still so thankful to be in the quietness of peace although it is a quiet bubbling with domestic and international problems. All problems find a solution, given the wisdom of their people, and I do feel that we have learned wisdom – learned it through horror, fear, hunger and destruction.

I do hope that you both are well and enjoying the cool autumn weather. How do the new teeth feel, Mother? You must have a photograph taken with a broad revealing grin so that we can see the new acquisitions. I hope you continue to sleep and eat well, Papa, and that your days are happy ones. Ronald and the children said to send you their love when I wrote today. Lee said to tell Papa that he will write him a long letter the next free weekend. He did appreciate so your letter, the stick of gum (which he shared with Susan) and all the things you told him.

Keep care of yourselves – our daily prayers and best wishes are for your health and happiness.

Affectionately, Yours,
Elisabeth

Cutting enclosed with letter (1945);
Headed 'In Great Britain nearly everybody reads the Daily Express'

Stretching it

The new clothing coupons are out today. are 24 of them, but they have to last till next April – eight months instead of the usual six.
If a man has two coupons left over from the last issue, he can "blue" the lot on a non-austerity suit (26 coupons) or he can have an austerity suit (20 coupons) and one sleeveless pullover (4), or a pair of slacks (8), a suit of pyjamas (8), and one shirt with collars and a tie (8)
A woman can buy a winter coat (18), leaving her with six coupons for all other clothing.
Or she can have two woollen dresses (22), and one pair of gloves (2). A pair of full-fashioned stockings a month leave nothing at all for anything else.
It's not much is it?

Same old shortage

Now what is the cause of this worse-than-wartime clothing scarcity?

The same old trouble – shortage of manpower and womanpower, aggravated in the case of the cotton-spinning industry by out-of-date conditions in the mills.
Well, speed up the reforms. Never let it be said that one section of the community let down the others. Never let hope be lost that better times can be brought about, even when things look bad.

Short notice

During the war the cloth manufacturers of Britain were able to produce prodigious quantities of material to clothe, not only their own armies, but the millions of American troops quartered in this country.
They have made millions more suits – including clerical outfits for the padres – to dress the troops on demobilisation better than disbanded armies have ever been dressed before.
If those highly-specialised clothing feats can be done at a few months' notice, there is no reason to doubt the capacity of the industry now.

Letter Thirty-Four

Moray Lodge
25 Newark Drive

Nov. 16, 1945

Dear Mother and Papa:

It seems quite a long time since there was a letter from either or both of you. I hope that the reason is merely diversion of interest and not illness. If you are like us, winter has set in with a determination after a prolonged Indian summer. There is snow up in the highlands of Scotland and it is cold enough for it here, and the children are praying that it comes for Christmas.

I am enclosing some snaps that were taken of the children when they went on a Loch Lomond steamer trip in the summer. They were taken by the American men in the photographs, and were recently sent on by one of them. Lee and Susan must have impressed them because not only did they send the snaps but also some candy and chewing gum, to say nothing of a box of marbles. Although the Americans have now sailed for the States, Lee has written to them to thank them; he was so overcome by their unsolicited kindness. The other little boy in the picture is Gordon Simpson who attends Kelvinside Academy with Lee.

I am in the midst of making Susan's birthday for Dec. 8, when she will be seven. I have made her a large stuffed doll standing almost three feet high, and have dressed it with a complete wardrobe made out of oddments, from old curtains to old hats. Ronald is buying her a canary as she has long been asking for one, and "when the war is over" can no longer be used as an excuse. She will have her usual party, for which I have been trying to save from our meagre rations. It must be grand to be a child again and live for birthdays.

Ronald and I took Lee to the big International football game last Saturday when 90,000 gathered in the huge Mammoth Hampden ground. He did enjoy it and spent most of his time explaining soccer to two American soldiers who sat behind him.

The children and I have been enjoying playing duets, very simple but very effective on the piano. Susan has a remarkable touch and memory, while Lee reads very freely, although his touch is heavy. Mary, our maid, sings all the time and Susan in a Scottish voice almost as good as Mary's has a grand time learning all her songs.

I went to the theatre last night to see Flaubert's' Madam Beauveria, while Ronald went to his club where there was a gathering of all of Scotland's foremost artists. Glasgow is very alive culturally and one seems so much a part of it, far more so than one did in London.

We listened to Attlee's speech to Congress and were struck by his frankness and wondered how he appealed to the American public.

Last week I received a package from Dorothy Hart Gifford containing a splendid costume and blouse, both of which I appreciated. I have recently had to invest in winter underclothing for all the family and that has eaten up practically the whole year's coupons. There is still very little in the shops to buy even if one had the coupons, because most of the manufacturers are doing demob work and the civilians have to wait. They tell us also that 75 per cent of what is manufactured for civilians is going to overseas trade. One often wishes that gloves, hose, stockings, shirts and all the little things grew on trees.

Mother and Father Bradbury had a safe and pleasant run back to Derbyshire and felt all the better for their two weeks' stay with us. They both were looking much better than last year and in much better spirits.

You never mentioned whether the treatment for little Martha's mark was eventually successful (not successfully). I do wish that Susan could see her. Last week we were at some friends whose sister was staying with them. She had just been presented with a set of twin boys. Susan's joy at seeing them and helping to feed one of them was without bounds.

I do wish that I could send you and the rest of the family some Christmas remembrance, but the situation still does not permit it. Someday perhaps I can send some souvenirs of Scotland that will make up for all your presents of the past years.

It is now time for me to go down into the town for shopping. Glasgow is a good shopping centre when, and if, conditions improve.

Do take care of yourselves in this cold winter weather and live your days in warm, luxurious content. All four of us send you our love and kisses and the children say that they will write you each a nice long letter in the coming holidays.

    Affectionately, your
    Elisabeth

Chapter Four - Post-War Articles
PIECE FROM ELISABETH BRADBURY (NO TIME FOR TEARS)

No Time for Tears

It was New York – and it was summer – and best of all it was America. No talking, however much, could explain to the children the thrill of America in reality. For the eight day trip over on the troop ship I had hammered out to them all they should expect to find in New York, but nothing I had said seemed adequate.

We had landed on the Saturday but could not begin our long journey out to the Middle west until we had visited the travel agency on the Monday. We had to make sure of our passage back to Scotland, before we could let ourselves go in America.

On the Sunday we did all the usual things, visiting Grant's Tomb, Riverside Church, International House and Columbia as tribute to my sojourn among them many years ago. In the afternoon, at the children's request we went to Bronx Zoo. The London Zoo had been one of their favourite jaunts when we lived there during the war, but the Bronx Zoo seemed more alive to them. Perhaps they could enjoy the animals without the fear of flying bombs.

The panda drew Susan, and she stopped in front of a stall selling panda toy bears. She, who had been starved for 'shop toys' during the war, wanted a large replica of the Giant panda. I tried to explain how our money was very limited, as we were only allowed to take so little out of Britain, and that that little must see us to Oklahoma and back again to Scotland. I managed to convince her that if we spent money foolishly on toys we should not have enough money either to eat with or to get home again.

For one of seven years, she understood quite well, but she did not appreciate her Brother's sentiment when he said, "You should not be so greedy as to want a toy for yourself, when you know we haven't much money".

Enough said, and tomorrow was another day. Early on the Monday we visited the Travel Agency and did our business, then we explored Rockefeller Centre. Susan's face was rapidly becoming longer and longer and she registered misery in every pore. I knew what was the matter: the shops were crammed full of toys that cried out for her to buy. She was determined that after the Panda episode, she wouldn't even ask. She stuck to her guns.

Rain descended in worse deluges than I had ever seen. A Fifth Ave. bus drew up and we boarded it, sitting in two seats facing each other – Susan resting against me and Lee on the opposite seat. There were two smartly dressed ladies beside us. Susan smiled, and one of the ladies smiled back, opened her purse and offered Susan a stick of gum. Susan halved it with Lee.

The lady then opened her purse again and gave her the whole package of gum. The ball started rolling, when Susan said her "thank you".

"Where did you get your rosy cheeks? California?" the lady asked.
"No Scotland!" Susan replied.
"When did you arrive?"
"Saturday"
"Has your Mother taken you to the big toy shop on Fifth Ave.?"
"No, we can't go!" answered Susan with grim determination.

The lady turned to me in amazement and I had to explain sketchily the position: that I thought it would be cruel to take a desiring child who had been denied toys for seven years, into a shop crammed full of toys when I was in the unfortunate position of not being able to gratify her desire.

The lady understood, and I trusted that she saw the logic of my reasoning. I was trying to be kind to Susan, not cruel. Before I knew what happened, I felt something thrust into my hand, and heard the lady across saying:
"You're to take these two children to the toy shop on Fifth Ave. and buy them a toy from me."

I opened my mouth to speak …

"There is no refusing. It's my gift to them. I can do this for them, when they have done so much for me."

My mouth no longer tried to convey my words; my heart did it instead. It burst and the tears came flooding from my eyes. I was ashamed and tried to hide them, but I could not stop them. My hand limply clutched the ten dollar bill.

The other lady beside me spoke,
"Come, this is no time for tears. With all you must have gone through during the war, you mustn't cry about a little thing like this."

Indeed it was no time for tears. I had been dry-eyed through all of London's bombing and England's endurance, but now my eyes were flooded – flooded through the kind generosity of a stranger to my children.

The voice beside me continued,

"My husband manufactures skates. I would be pleased if you would let me send each of the children a pair of skates, wherever they are going."

I could not refuse. The sincerity of her voice drew out the address from me. The bus stopped, and we were at our destination. My eyes were dry then, but when I looked down at Susan her so-blue eyes were veiled in tears.

"And why are you crying, my young lady?" I asked.

She pulled me down to her height and whispered,

"But don't you understand. Those ladies were an answer to my prayer last night. When Lee had teased me about being greedy at the Zoo and wanting a Panda bear, I asked God last night in my prayers to make me not a greedy little girl. Now those ladies have made it so that I don't have to be greedy."
The mist that then swam before my eyes was as great as the mist which blotted out the towering Empire State above.

The story should end there, but there is a sequel.

There was nothing to be done, but there and then we found our way to the Fifth Ave. toy shop mentioned by the ladies, and we entered to buy the toys. I cannot describe the children's reactions. Susan stood wide-eyed with wonder. She went from one showcase to another. I knew that her decision would be a long one, so at her suggestion we left her and Lee and I went upstairs to find the boy's toys. What a time Susan was going to have! The ground floor was nothing but dolls, and she had five dollars to spend.

When we came down later, Susan was surrounded by attendants. One said, "Your daughter wants a doll, but she says that she has only five dollars and we're afraid we have nothing that price. They are all more expensive."

The longing, hurt look in Susan's eyes could hardly be borne.

"it's all right," I said. "Thanks for your trouble with her. I'll have to take her elsewhere less expensive."

"But the lady on the bus said this shop. Oh, it must be this shop – her shop!" pleaded Susan.

The attendants looked at me for explanation. I had to explain and out came the story of the fairy-godmother and the ten dollar bill.

"So you see," I ended "she really has only five dollars."

The manageress then spoke to Susan.

"I'm afraid there has been a mistake. Will you come with me?" She held out her hand and Susan went with her. They went to a big showcase, and the manageress drew out a beautiful little doll. She went to another case and took out a miniature band-box and filled it with three dresses (each marked one dollar seventy-five), three hats, gloves, little socks and shoes, and a small hand-bag. She placed them neatly into the band-box, tied a red ribbon around it then handed both the doll and the box to bewildered Susan.

She made out a bill for five dollars, then turned.

"That will be five dollars and five cents for tax. You do have five cents?" There was a twinkle in her eye.

I did – I was wealthy – I had more than five cents. I had the knowledge that children believed in prayers, and that grown-ups believed in children!

Chapter Five
'SO YOU'RE AN AMERICAN!'

I was and I am, although I am married to an Englishman. This unique double nationality is possible thanks to the generosity of the American legislature. America is the only country that has seen fit to say to its women "If you marry an Englishman, you may be his in name but you are ours in spirit because you were born an American." In other words to those wondering American women, 'once an American always an American'.

This wise and judicious granting is for the best, for with an American birth and education, with the characteristics and manners of the American nation bred into one, he can hardly take off his cloak of nationality by merely marrying a 'foreigner'. He may change the maker's tab on his coat, but never its texture nor its design. This I have found to be true. I need only to speak or to venture and 'Un-English' viewpoint and I am greeted with the remark "So you're an American."

I am and I am proud of it. It's not only a great country to live in but it is a splendid one to be from. Not everyone will agree with you. English people, most of them that is, have queer ideas of Americans, and there is much combatting or former opinions and altering of ideas that you have to do. It's like being a social missionary to some extent, converting them to the correct knowledge and belief of Americans.

This converting is not so easy as it seems for their already formed idea of us is hard to change. They have formed their conception of an American from several sources: the films, our literature, newspaper clippings about us, our magazines that creep over here, previous knowledge of a visiting American, and last and the rarest, a visit to America.

Of these means of knowing us, the average Englishman gets his greatest idea from the movies or cinema. We are a mad race so he thinks. We spend so much time doing things quickly that there is never any time to do anything. Logical, isn't it? As for our women, they are beautiful, wise and dumb at the same time, tyrants over their men, and almost wholly without rhyme, reason or morals. The men are business drivers, usually thick set with horn-rim glasses, chewing the eternal cigar, rushing through the day at a hectic pace and not so straight in their dealings. Our children respect their parents. Of course there are variations and exceptions to these - but this is one conception that I have found prevalent.

As for our American laws, there are many made but many many more broken. Gangsters run wild all the time, kidnapping faces every child in the country, murders are personal experience, divorces are a matter of a daily routine.

Our American humour as seen on the movies is often too swift, too national for them, and too dumb. He may laugh, uproariously too, but in his opinion that joke is always capped by a better English one.

For the English audiences there are two types of films of America: the type that portrays our gangsters and makes heroes of them, the fast moving sophisticated sex-drama and a life of mad idiosyncrasies; the other type is the one that portrays the historical either in history or literature, and the combative forces. Of the latter take G-Men. It was a grand picture, well up in the opinion of the movie officials and certainly constructive in its viewpoint of what the government is doing to fight the bad men of America. Yet as I walked out of the theatre after seeing this, I heard many comments like this: What an awful place America is to have such crime. They think that every American citizen is either a gangster or one who is confronted with them. The murders in the States are more frequent and more horrible than any anywhere. Yet I, one of these cold blooded murder educated Americans has been shocked by the Ravine murders, the trunk murders that have occurred in England in the past two years.

But back to the films, one night I had seen a good show, which should have been a good advertisement to America. During the interval between the shows I overheard my neighbor ask the friend with whom he was sitting just how he liked the show.

"Too dammed Yankee," he replied. And there lies the trouble! Too dammed Yankee! They enjoy our films, go to see them in preference to the stolid English ones, yet criticise them because they are American. As for the word Yankee it is applied to anything American. As for the origin and significance of the word there is not the slightest knowledge. How I would like to hear a Southern Colonel explain (with gestures) the difference and pure meaning of the word Yankee.

The knowledge the average Englishman gathers from the films about his American friends, is augmented by the general idea he picks up about us from the modern literature that finds its way over here - and most of it does. You can get practically any American book that you see fit to desire, and the lending libraries will tell you that American novels are greatly in demand. Western stories open up a new field to the imagination of Britain, mystery and murder stories are much the same the world over but American ones seem to impress the most. As for fiction other than western and mystery-murder, a great deal is read. Why? To know about Americans? Hardly! One friend, when I saw she was reading an American novel, replied when I asked her why, "There are always so many nice descriptions of women and their clothes in your American books."

It was shortly after I came over to live. I was out to tea and another guest kept staring at me. Near the end of the afternoon I felt like saying, "Haven't you ever seen an American close-up before?" and was just on the verge of doing so when she ventured to say "You are not at all like Ann Vickers." It was the latest American book (or perhaps the only one) she had read and generalising was no crime to her.

But literature isn't all the reading they do about America - the newspaper articles are priceless in portraying American life. Such sub-titles as 'Judge who hit man out', 'Film star divorces fifth husband' and similar ones call forth great mirth. America must be a free and easy place to live.

The magazines are of two sorts: the acceptable ones that are an asset and second the low love or detective type. Of the former, it is surprising how many are read. In our section of England, in the North Country in a sea-side place, a man walked into my husband's office carrying a Reader's Digest. My husband was curious to know how he happened to have the magazine. He saw one in London and got them ever since - they told you a lot about America that some of the others didn't. Household magazines for women are prevalent though it is more apt to be the English edition of the American magazines. The

English woman likes our ads; they intrigue her.

The low type of magazines is heralded on the stalls of the market places as 'Yankee - or Yank -magazines' and they are of the lowest degree possible. Yet they have a brisk trade.

The American who comes to England on a visit is another means by which the Englishman may judge Americans. This is perhaps one of the best source for judgement, because they can see for themselves what we look like and how we talk and if they care to listen they may find out something that will contradict their idea of what America is. Yet they are prone to look down upon the visiting American because he is a tourist - one who comes ravaging to England. They come to the English galleries, guide book in hand and wander through bored-like, saying at the end that they have done the art gallery.

An idea of what impression a visiting American can make on one, I quote the following book passage, written by an English woman. The speech was put into the mouth of a Frenchman in the story but it was but a veiled putting. A shop keeper was asked if an American had come into his shop and what he looked like:

"He was just an American. His voice was in his nose. He could not speak French. He was chewing gum. He had tortoise-shell glasses. He was tall, and I think, not very old."

"Would you know him if you saw him again?"

"I could not say. So many Americans come and go. He was not remarkable in any way."

If the Englishman is lucky enough he may have visited America. However that is no criterion that his conception of America is going to be on a higher and more complimentary level -more often not. For example I recently heard the following talk over the radio by an Englishman who had just returned from the States and was trying to educate the younger generation as to what America was like: "The people are ruthless and infinitely boring. They are divided into two types: men and women. The men are horn rimmed, chew gum and talk business better and better. The women spend their time fixing their hair and reading books on psychology. Americans are all one - they are united on their ideals which are proving false. Freedom doesn't exist, opportunity is crushed out by the depression and the idea of equality has led to too much standardisation." This was his talk. However at the end fearing that some Americans might be listening he added, as a sort of postscript,

"The Americans are kind and good-hearted and lead an exciting and stimulating life." The afterthought was generous to say the least.
I know of nothing that angers and riles me so much as to read a book written by an English man who has spent six weeks or two months in the States and thinks he is the super-divine critic of America. It is not so much what he says, but how he says it. He has accepted American hospitality and yet derides the fact that his friends over there were overzealous about the success of his journey. He tries always to score off America, without playing ball with her. Seeing New York isn't seeing America, seeing Hollywood isn't seeing the romance of the country. It is a vast place; if the Englishman wants to write about it, let him live there for three years at least, not visit there for three weeks. A little knowledge is a dangerous thing.

Now that I have covered the sources of American propaganda that reaches the staunch British shores, I might well ask the question, "Do the English like the Americans?" I don't mean as a nation, as a social whole, but rather as a personal character or individuals. They either do or they don't; they will be true supporters or sour critics. To those who like us I may say that they are broad-minded, far-sighted, open to suggestion and give credit where credit is due. As for those who hated us, why should they do so. It is rather in-bred and easily explainable. America to the narrow-minded Britisher is still the angry, obstinate child who awkwardly gained her independence. She has no stamina of her own - is weak and wobbly in her foundation and her ideals. She has grown and progressed, but it is a wild progression without aim. If you meet the latter type of Englishman it is almost impossible to make him see any good points wither in America or in her people. For instance, my husband was asked to address the Rotary Club on the subject of America. He did so gladly, presenting it in the light that the average Englishman would appreciate. At the end he was tendered a vote of thanks that turned out to be more like a vote of censure. The speaker said,
"Before coming to this meeting today, I never liked America, and I like it far less now."
Another time I was playing bridge. My partner was noticeably rude in her remarks and attitude when she found out that I was an American. At the end of the afternoon, my hostess apologised to me, saying that

Mrs. A. had a mental phobia about Americans. It seems her only brother took all his money (very little at that) and went to America where he had high hopes of making a fortune. He had to cable home for money to come home, as he had lost everything. The woman after that blamed America – not her mad brother - for the failure and loss of his expedition.

This next part is a part-repeat of an earlier paragraph.
To the average Englishman we are a set type. Read the following excerpt from a recent popular English novel: "He was just an American. His voice was in his nose. He could not speak French. He was chewing the gum. He had tortoise-shell glasses. He was tall, and I think not very old."
"Would you know him if you saw him again?"
"I could not say. So many Americans come and go. He was not remarkable in any way."

These words were put into the mouth of a Frenchman, but they were definitely germinated in the mind of an Englishman. It is nothing more than a social punch in the nose.

I was fishing in Scotland with my father-in-law. We were staying in the hills. The heavy mist came on one evening early so we downed our rods and went to the village hop on the mountain-side. Every other dance was a Scottish version of bodily expression. They fascinated me. However, I was startled out of my contemplation of the fascination when a young Scottish youth asked me if I would dance one with him. I said I didn't know it, but my denial seemed to make little difference as he vowed that all I need do was to follow him. So follow him I set out to do. After some thirty spins with his finger on my head, some twirls about, and this repeated incessantly for twenty minutes, I was well on to the state of complete collapse. I asked him if he would mind if I gave up the struggle as I felt ill. He looked at me very oddly.
"You're American aren't you?"
"Yes"
"Well, I thought Americans were tough." Perhaps I was supposed to be tough but all signs of toughness were absent as I slunk to my wall-seat. No, they have no fear of putting us all in one category. They fail to realise that we are all human beings, prone to differ as Englishmen.

How ignorant they are of us? Some of the questions put to me sound daft but have been quite genuine. Are American Indians red? Do university degrees mean anything or can you get them by merely applying for them as you would a license? Do you have any religion in America or are you in the same trend as Russia? What is a fraternity that you hear about?

Yes, their questions are many and varied. They cannot visualize either our country or our life. The vastness of our land is incomprehensible to them. Our sky-scrapers are un-heard of monstrosities that defy the rhyme and beauty of nature. Our co-educational universities and schools cannot possibly turn out educated men and women.

They have much to learn about us. Some Englishmen want to learn and a few are given the opportunity to do so through scholarships and travel in the States. Even fewer take time off to study and live our life instead of taking a bird's eye view. But, if their ideas of us are queer, it is we who have planted the seeds for those ideas with our movies, our books, our tourists and our newspapers. They sprinkle these seeds with their Nordic imagination, cold crisp and scanty as it is. I can't say whether they like us or not. Give them time to know us and they can't deny us a fair test. However, it is hard trying to give them the time and opportunity to know us properly. We Americans are few and far between over here, and at that they can't judge a myriad nation from a few individuals.

So you're an American. In the face of all this, I still say, "Yes, and proud of it."

Chapter Six
A Sooner Born 2

"So you're from Oklahoma!" Her voice was incredulous and the look on her face one of sudden discovery.
"Yes." I replied. "Is that hard to believe?"
"Perhaps not, she said, "but your eyes aren't on the slant."
I could have told her the difference between Yokohama and Oklahoma, but I didn't.

When people first meet me and realize that I am from Oklahoma, they fall into three categories in my mind. Those who are jumbled and doubtful about the whereabouts of it; those who know all about it from films, books, or musicals, and those who say, "Tell me what it's really like. I have no idea."

Into the first category falls the lady of the first instance, and another whom I met at one of my Mother-in-law's village meetings, and exclaimed, "But you are not a red-Indian or a cow-girl!"

Into the second category comes the very superior demoiselle whom I met at an exclusive dance in Glasgow. "So you're from Oklahoma! You must be an Oakie - Grapes of Wrath. Remember?" I wanted to tell her that Steinbeck's careful portrayal could have been placed in any of the dust-bowl states, and that the social, economic problem he was putting across could have been that of Kansas and Texas as well as of Oklahoma. But instead, I called it quits with, "And you are from Glasgow! No Mean City. Remember?"

Into the third category come also those film addicts and cowboy worshippers. When the land girl on the farm where we were staying in Wales this summer, heard that my son had been to Oklahoma, had met Roy Rogers, and actually seen him working on location on a ranch ---- even he became a hero in her eyes. And when my son told her about Gene Autry buying a derelict and deserted small town in

Oklahoma and turning it into the now alive "Gene Audrey, Oklahoma" - that was better still!

In this group I also class those who say, "So you're from Oklahoma. You must see Oklahoma when you go to London." I want to say that I decided against seeing it three years ago in New York, chiefly because I was from Oklahoma. However, I must admit that I took my daughter to see it this Easter in London, so that we both could say when told we must see it, "WE HAVE SEEN IT!" That is so much easier than trying to explain why we don't care to see Oklahoma.

In the third category, I place all those people who say , "So you're from Oklahoma. What is it really like? Tell me about when you were little there. How civilized is it now? What are the people like?" If I have time, I start to tell them.

Geographically speaking Oklahoma lies on top of Texas, like the top section of a double boiler - the pan handles of both states sliding into one another. As for Texas, it embraces the Gulf of Mexico. Some geologists maintain that one of the oldest ranges of mountain in the United States is the Arbuckle Mountain which runs through Oklahoma. These are not high in comparison with the Rockies but their strata and structure are unique. Sweeping down from these mountains are plains where corn tosses in the wind, cotton glistens in the sun - sweet potatoes, sugar cane, alfalfa and peanuts make up the ground crops - where peach orchards, pecan trees, persimmon groves and dogwood relieve the might-be, monotony of the prevalent scrub oak.

The landscape is now peppered with oil fields, discreetly designed and immaculately laid out compared to the first oil fields. In the midst of the skyscraper cities, Oklahoma City and Tulsa, you now find oil derricks and pumps pulsing beside the very life of the suburbia.

The weather in the summer is hot - mighty hot, as my Father would have said - and cold, mighty cold in the winter: but the summer takes nine months of the year and the winter only three. As children, our great dread was tornadoes, which swept up from the Gulf of Mexico and culred into magnificent fury across Texas and into Oklahoma. All the schools and most of the houses had store cellars ---- so air raid shelters were not so new to me during the war. However, in recent years the tornadoes have decreased in number, and the dust storms have taken over. These began because the great stretches of plain were robbed of their goodness, the soil corroded and a small wind carried a little dust, grew larger and in the end a huge dust storm blackened out your town, entered your sealed windows and literally stopped your daily existence. These menaces are now being combatted by careful rotation of crops, planting of breaker forests, and returfing of the cattle chewed ranges.

The humidity of the southern part of Oklahoma has changed from dry to very humid, stifling heat in the summer because of the recent building of two large lakes: the smaller one Lake Murray (named after a governor of the state) and the very large Lake Texoma which stretches from up in Oklahoma down into Texas. These man-made lakes have offered great sporting and relaxation facilities to the people of these two states. Historically speaking, Oklahoma is one of the most interesting states in the Union. It is commonly known as the Sooner State and began its life as Indian Territory. The story is a long one ---- back to the days when the five civilized tribes (the Chickasaws, Choctaws, Cherokees, Creeks and Seminoles: so-called civilized because they were more advanced than some of the other Indian tribes) were ousted from their Eastern homes with the promise from the government that they be given a strip of land in the middle west. They moved west and were given a concession of land with other local tribes, north of Texas. Where they would supposedly be at peace and undisturbed by the White Man, but the Civil War came and pioneers who had lost their all in the South moved westward and joined the Indians. These White Settlers agitated for the Opening of a strip of Indian Territory to White Settlers.

President Harrison on April 22, 1889 opened a strip of 20,000 white settlers who lined the homestead settlement. They lined the borders of the strip and at the crack of a pistol they raced forward to claim their homestead – but some were cleverer than others and got there sooner than the rest. Hence the name of the Sooner State.

The numerous territories began to take shape, form townships and organize government. In 1890 they were organized officially into the Territory of Oklahoma ---- Oklahoma being the Choctaw word meaning red people. In this combined territory along with the white settlers were the local tribes: the Kowa, Comanche and Apache, with the remnants of other tribes crowded in: Choctaws, Chickasaws,

Cherokees, Creeks, Seminoles, Osages, Kaws, Poncas, Cheyenne's, Iowa's, Kickapoos, Shawnees, Ottawa's and others. On the 17th of November 1907 the Territory was admitted into the Union as the State of Oklahoma.

My Father had pioneered into this country when his family had been rendered homeless and penniless by Sherman's March to the Sea. The old plantation had nothing left for a young youth, and he joined his older brothers as they moved west. They were the engineers of that new country. They built roads, bridges, dams, building, schools and railways. The history of the state of Oklahoma is the history of their lives.

In 1909 into a small community in Southern Oklahoma I joined our already swollen family, as its youngest member. Years later when I wanted my first passport to Europe, my Father and the old doctor who had delivered me, had to go before the Registrar and swear that I was born, for there had been no written record of my birth.

In those days, my home could have been called a board town, for practically everything was built of boards: the shops, the houses, the schools, the churches, the old open air opera house, and even the sidewalks. It is hard to believe that that was only forty years ago, for today there rears its head where that board town used to be ---- a modern city with wide paved streets, boulevards, skyscrapers, elegant homes, magnificent churches and outstanding schools. It was the guts of men like my Father who made it so. They had to work against odds. One year the whole town was razed to the ground by a tornado. The next year a big explosion from oil tankards on the railway blew the town sky high again ---- and still it was rebuilt.

The town was divided into four wards: first, second, third and fourth and from each ward came the representatives to the Chamber of Commerce from which was elected the Mayor. Each ward had its own grammar school which took the children from the age of six at the first grade until the age of twelve at the sixth grade. Then they left the grammar school and went into the big Junior High School which catered for all the children of the town from the seventh through the ninth grade. If successful, they then passed onto the Senior High School. There were no private or fee-paying schools. There were city schools for all the people, rich and poor alike; the sons of the mayor sat down beside the daughters of the oil field worker. The only segregation was the natural one that takes place in any town: better families living in one district and less fortunate ones in others, but even this segregation was completely lost when the children met in the Junior and Senior schools. There was one exception: the negroes had their own schools, as thorough and adequate as the whites ---- but in their section of the town known commonly as negro town.

I had always been conscious of negroes as part of the background of my youth. Presumably the Civil War had cut off the negroes from the white families and made them independent ---- but for many generations to come, they still found their life and interests among the life and interests of the white people. My Mother and Father were good to the negroes who worked for them and helped them in more ways than one. The negroes relied upon them for the stability of their lives as my parents relied upon them for the embellishments of their daily tasks. Much of my present philosophy of life I base upon that of Ole Bertha, our cook. The smells of fried chicken would draw me into the kitchen, where I would find Ole Bertha stirring cream gravy in a big skillet ---- her mammoth black-side following the movement of her stirring. If there was anything the matter with me, she would say, "Lawdsy, child - there ain't nothing worth frettin' over. Don't you fret." She didn't and she always got there smiling.

The churches were literally the social centers of the town for on week days there was so much to be done just to live in this pioneering country ---- that when the Sabbath came, the people gave themselves wholeheartedly to it. At nine o'clock there was Sunday School, for the grown-ups as well as the youngsters. This got out about quarter to eleven, when the morning service was held. Here the personality of the minister held the congregation spell-bound. He was as tough and demanding as the lives they were living ---- and they admired him. What were the churches? The Methodist, Presbyterian, Episcopal, Christian, Catholic, Christian Scientist, Seven Day Adventist ---- and any other sect that had enough followers to get together. But the church life did not end with the Sunday all day services: there were sewing bees, Wednesday evening prayer meetings, monthly suppers, picnics and all manner of social occasions. The people lived their church and their religion!

Holidays were unheard of things in those early days. There was so much to be done that time off for gallivantin' didn't come around. But I won't say that they didn't play; they did. There was Thanksgiving, Christmas, New Year's, Washington's Birthday, Fourth of July and others. On such hey-days, we went out seeking beauty spots: Turner Falls with its cascades of water hiding caves behind; Buzzards Roost with boulders as big as houses; Blue Hole, where the swimming was as magic as the water, where the smell of the sulphur made you distrust every egg for weeks after; and Chickasaw Lake, where the fish asked to be caught.

What an event the County Fair was! There was always a rodeo with the town's chief bronco-busters, and the cow girls giving thrills every turn. There was judging of the horses and cattle ----and the tedious judging of Aunt Emma's dill pickle and of Aunt Bess' watermelon rind preserves ---- Uncle Ezra's silken corn-on-the-cob and Grandpa's black eyed peas. It usually ended up with a huge barbecue with long, wooden tables lining the barbecue pits where steaks, chickens, and hams roasted on their spits.

Those days seem a very long time ago, and Oklahoma seems a very long way away, but however old I become, and however far removed I find myself, I'll always carry in my heart that old tune:

I'm a Sooner born,
I'm a Sooner bred,
And when I die
I'll be a Sooner dead!

Epilogue

Betty and Ronald Bradbury at civic function in Liverpool in the 1950s

The Liverpool Echo, Monday, November 15, 1971

City's planning overlord dies

Dr. Ronald Bradbury, Liverpool Corporation's Director of Land and Property Services, and formerly city architect and director of housing died on Saturday, aged 63. He had been ill for several months.

Dr Bradbury, who leaves a widow and two married children, came to Liverpool in 1948 as successor to Sir Lancelot Keay, at a time when the city's post-war housing drive had not really begun in earnest.

The number of permanent homes built in 1947 was fewer than a thousand, but during fifteen years until Dr Bradbury's department was split up and he became city architect in 1963, the average number rose to 2,000-a-year despite a shortage of land.

One of Dr Bradbury's first tasks in Liverpool on arriving from his post as Director of Housing for Glasgow, was the completion of the Speke estate. This was followed by such major housing projects as the Croxteth estate, Deysbrook Lane, Childwall Valley, Lee Park, Macket's Lane and Halewood.

But the major event was the building of Kirkby where 10,000 dwellings were provided in the period from 1952 to 1960, and eventually Kirkby Urban District Council was formed.

Dr Bradbury's home was "The White House", South Road, Grassendale.

Ronald Bradbury died in 1971.

Elisabeth- Betty Bradbury, lived in a granny flat added on to the White House in 1972 , with Sue Newton (nee Susan Bradbury) and Alan Newton and their children Tim, Jenny and Christopher, till in 1992 the Newton family designed and built the Court House on the tennis court next door with a granny flat on the ground floor. Granny (Elisabeth) lived with the Newton family till she died in 1999.

She remained American till the end- she never took British citizenship, and took great pride in her American roots and values.

Elisabeth (Granny) with daughter Sue and grandaughter Jenny at the Court House.

Lee's Family

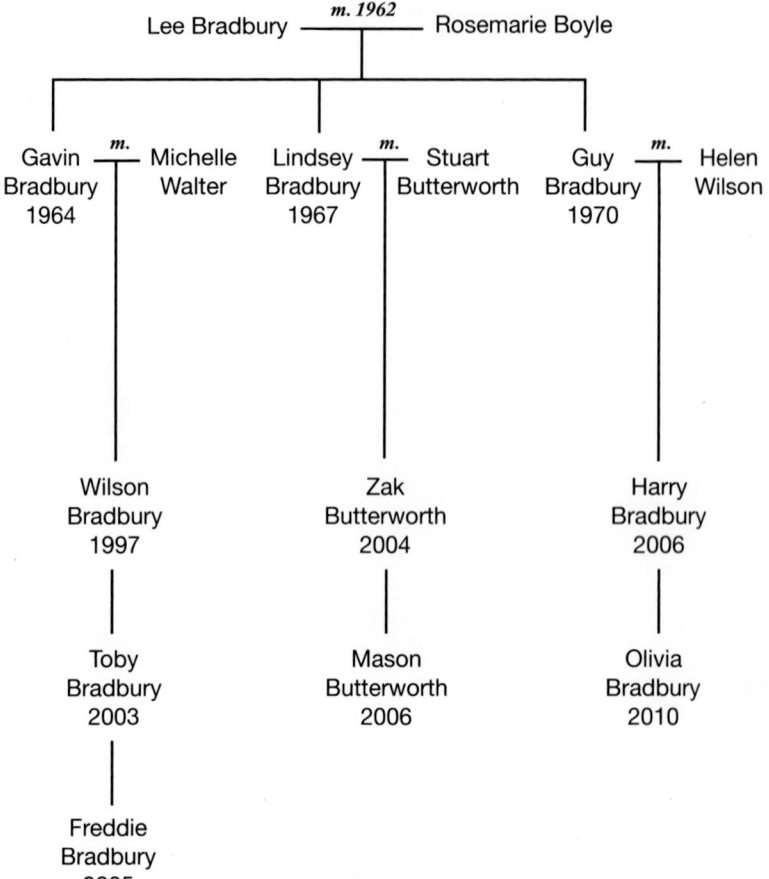

Susan's Family

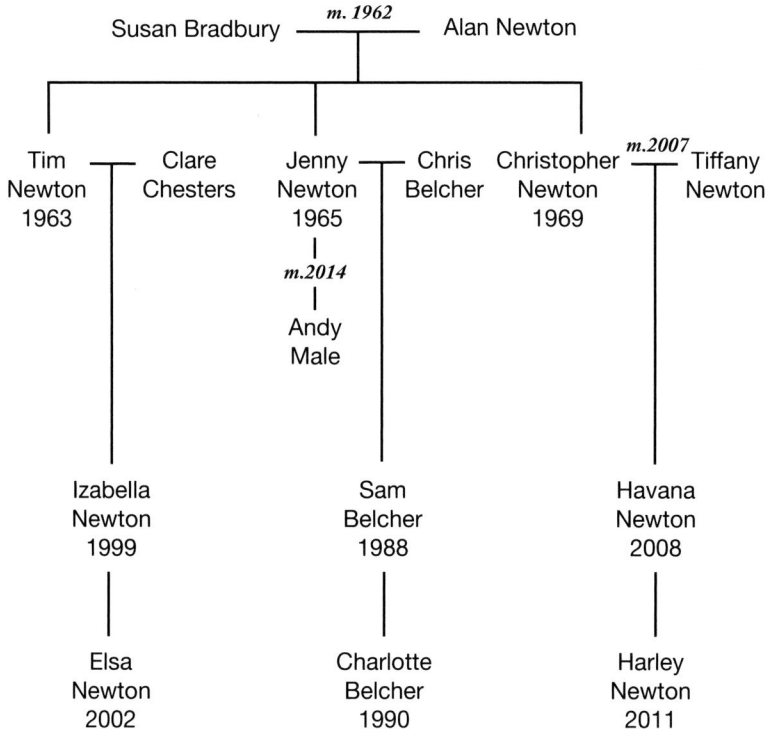

My thanks to everyone who has contributed
to the compiling of this book.
Pat Mew for deciphering my Mother's hand writing
and typing all of the letters - a major task.
Izabella Newton, my Granddaughter, for assisting
me in compiling the book and being sub- editor.
Chris Newton, my son, for organising and arranging
all the photographical material in the book, and
Alan my husband for his continuing
support and encouragement.
Sue Newton.